NIST Special Publication 800-175A

Guideline for Using Cryptographic Standards in the Federal Government:
Directives, Mandates and Policies

Elaine Barker
William C. Barker

This publication is available free of charge from:
http://dx.doi.org/10.6028/NIST.SP.800-175A

COMPUTER SECURITY

National Institute of
Standards and Technology
U.S. Department of Commerce

NIST Special Publication 800-175A

Guideline for Using Cryptographic Standards in the Federal Government:
Directives, Mandates and Policies

Elaine Barker
Computer Security Division
Information Technology Laboratory

William C. Barker
Domestic Guest Researcher
Information Technology Laboratory

This publication is available free of charge from:
http://dx.doi.org/10.6028/NIST.SP.800-175A

August 2016

U.S. Department of Commerce
Penny Pritzker, Secretary

National Institute of Standards and Technology
Willie May, Under Secretary of Commerce for Standards and Technology and Director

Authority

This publication has been developed by NIST in accordance with its statutory responsibilities under the Federal Information Security Modernization Act of 2014, 44 U.S.C. § 3551 *et seq.*, Public Law (P.L.) 113-283. NIST is responsible for developing information security standards and guidelines, including minimum requirements for federal information systems, but such standards and guidelines shall not apply to national security systems without the express approval of appropriate federal officials exercising policy authority over such systems. This guideline is consistent with the requirements of the Office of Management and Budget (OMB) Circular A-130.

Nothing in this publication should be taken to contradict the standards and guidelines made mandatory and binding on federal agencies by the Secretary of Commerce under statutory authority. Nor should these guidelines be interpreted as altering or superseding the existing authorities of the Secretary of Commerce, Director of the OMB, or any other federal official. This publication may be used by nongovernmental organizations on a voluntary basis and is not subject to copyright in the United States. Attribution would, however, be appreciated by NIST.

National Institute of Standards and Technology Special Publication 800-175A
Natl. Inst. Stand. Technol. Spec. Publ. 800-175A, 37 pages (August 2016)
CODEN: NSPUE2

This publication is available free of charge from:
http://dx.doi.org/10.6028/NIST.SP.800-175A

Certain commercial entities, equipment, or materials may be identified in this document in order to describe an experimental procedure or concept adequately. Such identification is not intended to imply recommendation or endorsement by NIST, nor is it intended to imply that the entities, materials, or equipment are necessarily the best available for the purpose.

There may be references in this publication to other publications currently under development by NIST in accordance with its assigned statutory responsibilities. The information in this publication, including concepts and methodologies, may be used by federal agencies even before the completion of such companion publications. Thus, until each publication is completed, current requirements, guidelines, and procedures, where they exist, remain operative. For planning and transition purposes, federal agencies may wish to closely follow the development of these new publications by NIST.

Organizations are encouraged to review all draft publications during public comment periods and provide feedback to NIST. Many NIST cybersecurity publications, other than the ones noted above, are available at http://csrc.nist.gov/publications.

Comments on this publication may be submitted to:

National Institute of Standards and Technology
Attn: Computer Security Division, Information Technology Laboratory
100 Bureau Drive (Mail Stop 8930) Gaithersburg, MD 20899-8930
Email: SP800-175@nist.gov

All comments are subject to release under the Freedom of Information Act (FOIA).

Reports on Computer Systems Technology

The Information Technology Laboratory (ITL) at the National Institute of Standards and Technology (NIST) promotes the U.S. economy and public welfare by providing technical leadership for the Nation's measurement and standards infrastructure. ITL develops tests, test methods, reference data, proof of concept implementations, and technical analyses to advance the development and productive use of information technology. ITL's responsibilities include the development of management, administrative, technical, and physical standards and guidelines for the cost-effective security and privacy of other than national security-related information in federal information systems. The Special Publication 800-series reports on ITL's research, guidelines, and outreach efforts in information system security, and its collaborative activities with industry, government, and academic organizations.

Abstract

This document is part of a series intended to provide guidance to the Federal Government for using cryptography and NIST's cryptographic standards to protect sensitive, but unclassified digitized information during transmission and while in storage. Special Publication (SP) 800-175A provides guidance on the determination of requirements for using cryptography. It includes a summary of laws and regulations concerning the protection of the Federal Government's sensitive information, guidance regarding the conduct of risk assessments to determine what needs to be protected and how best to protect that information, and a discussion of the relevant security-related documents (e.g., various policy and practice documents).

Keywords

authentication; confidentiality; critical infrastructure; cryptographic guideline; cryptography; Executive Orders; integrity; key management; laws; mandates; policy; Presidential Directives; risk assessment; standards.

Acknowledgments

The authors wish to thank the authors of NIST Special Publication (SP) 800-21 from which this document was derived, including Annabelle Lee, along with those colleagues that reviewed drafts of this document and contributed to its development. The authors also gratefully acknowledge and appreciate the many comments from the public and private sectors whose thoughtful and constructive comments improved the quality and usefulness of this publication.

Table of Contents

SECTION 1: INTRODUCTION

1.1 Background and Purpose

Cryptographic publications of the National Institute of Standards and Technology (NIST) provide guidance regarding how cryptographic protection is to be implemented, but do not specify when cryptographic protection is required. The decision regarding whether or not to employ cryptographic protection rests with the owner of the information to be protected. Decisions concerning the use of cryptographic protection are generally based on a thorough risk analysis that establishes the sensitivity of the information to be protected and the security controls that need to be used to protect that information, both during transmission and while in storage. This document provides guidance on the basis for determining requirements for using cryptography. It includes a summary of the laws, directives, standards, and guidelines concerning the protection of the Federal government's sensitive but unclassified information; guidance regarding the conduct of risk assessments to determine what information needs to be protected and how best to protect that information; and a discussion of application-relevant security documentation (e.g., various policy and practice documents). While the use of this guideline outside the Federal Government is strictly voluntary, many of the processes and references included herein may be useful in non-federal contexts.

The primary policy documents that apply to federal cryptographic systems include Public Laws, Presidential Executive Orders and Directives, and other guidance from Executive Office of the President organizations. Some Department of Commerce and NIST publications are identified in these policy documents as being mandatory for Federal organizations. Relevant NIST cryptographic publications are discussed in Special Publication (SP) 800-175B, *Guideline for Using Cryptographic Standards in the Federal Government: Cryptographic Mechanisms*.

1.2 Terms and Definitions

Authentication	As used in this document, a process that provides assurance of the source and integrity of information that is communicated or stored, or that provides assurance of an entity's identity.
Authorization	The official management decision given by a senior organizational official to authorize the operation of an information system and to explicitly accept the risk to organizational operations and assets, individuals, other organizations, and the Nation, based on the implementation of an agreed-upon set of security controls.
Breach	The loss of control, compromise, unauthorized disclosure, unauthorized acquisition, unauthorized access, or any similar term referring to situations where persons other than authorized users, or where authorized users take actions for an other than authorized purposes, have access or potential

	access to sensitive information, whether physical or electronic.
Categorization	The process of determining the security category for information or an information system. Security categorization methodologies are described in CNSS Instruction 1253 for national security systems and in FIPS Publication 199 for other than national security systems.
Ciphertext	Data in its encrypted form.
Confidentiality	The property that sensitive information is not disclosed to unauthorized entities.
Critical Infrastructure	The essential services that support a society and serve as the backbone for the society's economy, security and health.
Cryptographic algorithm	A well-defined computational procedure that takes variable inputs, including a cryptographic key (if applicable), and produces an output.
Cryptographic Key	A parameter used in conjunction with a cryptographic algorithm that determines its operation in such a way that an entity with knowledge of the key can reproduce or reverse the operation, while an entity without knowledge of the key cannot.
Cryptography	The science of information hiding and verification. It includes the protocols, algorithms and methodologies to securely and consistently prevent unauthorized access to sensitive information and enable verifiability of the information. The main goals include confidentiality, integrity authentication and source authentication.
Digital Infrastructure	The Digital Infrastructure is defined as the ability to store and exchange data through a centralized communication system. Data communication and exchange are all simplified with the right software and hardware equipment.
Encryption	The process of transforming plaintext into ciphertext for the purpose of security or privacy.
Entity	An individual (person), organization, device or process.
Executive Office of the President	The President's immediate staff, along with entities such as the Office of Management and Budget, the National Security Staff, the Office of Science and Technology Policy, and the Office of Personnel Management.
Executive Orders	Legally binding orders given by the President, acting as the head of the Executive Branch, to Federal Administrative Agencies. Executive Orders are generally used to direct

	federal agencies and officials in their execution of congressionally established laws or policies.
High Impact	The loss of confidentiality, integrity, or availability could be expected to have a severe or catastrophic adverse effect on organizational operations, organizational assets, or individuals.
Identity Management	Broadly refers to the administration of individual identities within a system, such as a company, a network or even a country. In enterprise IT, identity management is about establishing and managing the roles and access privileges of individual network users.
Integrity	The property that protected data has not been modified or deleted in an unauthorized and undetected manner.
Key Establishment	The procedure that results in keying material that is shared among different parties.
Keying Material	The data (e.g., keys) necessary to establish and maintain cryptographic keying relationships.
Key Management	The activities involving the handling of cryptographic keys and other related security parameters (e.g., counters) during the entire life cycle of the keys, including the generation, storage, establishment, entry and output, and destruction.
Low-Impact	The loss of confidentiality, integrity, or availability could be expected to have a limited adverse effect on organizational operations, organizational assets, or individuals.
Mandate	A mandatory order or requirement under statute.
Moderate Impact	The loss of confidentiality, integrity, or availability could be expected to have a serious adverse effect on organizational operations, organizational assets, or individuals.
Plaintext	Intelligible data that has meaning and can be understood without the application of cryptography.
Policy	The set of basic principles and associated guidelines, formulated and enforced by the governing body of an organization, to direct and limit its actions in pursuit of long-term goals.
Presidential Directive	A form of an executive order issued by the President of the United States with the advice and consent of the National Security Council; also known as a Presidential Decision Directive (or PDD).

Reciprocity	The mutual agreement among participating organizations to accept each other's security assessments in order to reuse information-system resources and/or to accept each other's assessed security posture in order to share information.
Risk Analysis	See risk assessment.
Risk Assessment	The process of identifying risks to organizational operations (including mission, functions, images, and reputation), organizational assets, individuals, other organizations, and the Nation, resulting from the operation of an information system. Part of risk management, incorporates threat and vulnerability analyses, and considers mitigations provided by security controls planned or in place.
Risk Management	The program and supporting processes to manage information security risk to organizational operations (including mission, functions, images, and reputation), organizational assets, individuals, other organizations, and the Nation, and includes: (i) establishing the context for risk-related activities, (ii) assessing risk, (iii) responding to risk once determined, and (iv) monitoring risk over time.
Security Control	A safeguard or countermeasure prescribed for an information system or an organization designed to protect the confidentiality, integrity, and availability of its information and to meet a set of defined security requirements.
Security Policy	A set of criteria for the provision of security services.
Security Strength	A number associated with the amount of work (that is, the number of operations) that is required to break a cryptographic algorithm or system.
Standard	A document that provides requirements, specifications, guidelines or characteristics that can be used consistently to ensure that materials, products, processes and services are fit for their purpose.
Two-Factor Authentication	Proof of the possession of a physical or software token in combination with some memorized secret knowledge.

1.3   Acronyms

CIO	Chief Information Officer
CNSS	Committee for National Security Systems
DHS	Department of Homeland Security
DNSSEC	Domain Name System Security Extensions
DOD	Department of Defense
EOP	Executive Office of the President
FIPS	Federal Information Processing Standard
FISMA	Federal Information Security Management Act (P.L. 107-347)
GSA	General Services Administration
HHS	Health and Human Services
HIPAA	Health Insurance Portability and Accountability Act
HITECH	Health Information Technology for Economic and Clinical Health
HSPD	Homeland Security Presidential Directive
IC	Intelligence Community
IG	Inspector General
IT	Information Technology
ITL	Information Technology Laboratory
JTFTI	Joint Task Force Transformation Initiative
NIST	National Institute of Standards and Technology
NISTIR	NIST Interagency or Internal Report
NPIVP	NIST Personal Identity Verification Program
NSC	National Security Council
ODNI	Office of the Director of National Intelligence
OMB	Office of Management and Budget
OPM	Office of Personnel Management
PHI	Protected Health Information
PIV	Personal Identity Verification
PKI	Public Key Infrastructure
P.L.	Public Law
SAOP	Senior Agency Official for Privacy
SP	Special Publication

U.S.C.   United States Code

1.4 Document Organization

This publication is organized as follows:

- Section 1 provides an introduction to this document, including its background and purpose, a definition of terms, and a list of acronyms used herein.

- Section 2 describes legislative mandates that are relevant to the cryptographic standards and guidelines that are developed by NIST, or in the development of which NIST participates.

- Section 3 discusses directives from the Executive Office of the President (EOP) that are relevant to cryptographic standards and guidelines that are developed by NIST, or in the development of which NIST participates.

- Section 4 provides a brief treatment of organization-specific policies that may prescribe the cryptographic services that need to be provided and the level of protection needed.

- Section 5 provides a brief treatment of the risk management process that determines security control requirements – including cryptographic requirements.

- Appendix A includes a list of references.

SECTION 2: APPLICABLE PUBLIC LAWS

This section describes elements of legislative mandates that are relevant to the cryptographic standards and guidelines that are developed by NIST, or in the development of which NIST participates.

2.1 E-Government Act of 2002 (FISMA)

Title III of Public Law 107-347 is cited as the Federal Information Security Management Act of 2002 (FISMA) and has been incorporated into Sections 20 and 21 of the NIST Act.

Paragraph 3543 of the Act provides for the Executive Office of the President to coordinate the development of standards and guidelines by the National Institute of Standards and Technology (NIST) (under Section 20 of the National Institute of Standards and Technology Act [15 U.S.C. 278g–3]) with agencies and offices operating or exercising control of national security systems (including the National Security Agency) to assure, to the maximum extent feasible, that such standards and guidelines are complementary with standards and guidelines developed for national security systems.

Section 302 of the Act directs the Secretary of Commerce (under Section 11331 of Title 40 United States Code (U.S.C.)) to prescribe standards and guidelines pertaining to federal information systems, based on standards and guidelines developed by NIST. Section 302 of the Act makes these standards compulsory and binding to the extent determined necessary by the Secretary to improve the efficiency of the operation or security of federal information systems, and also states that the standards shall include information security standards that—

(1) Provide minimum information security requirements as determined under Section 20(b) of the National Institute of Standards and Technology Act (15 U.S.C. 278g–3(b)); and

(2) Are otherwise necessary to improve the security of federal information and information systems.

Only the President is assigned the authority to disapprove or modify these standards.

The heads of executive agencies may employ standards for the cost-effective information security of information systems within or under the supervision of that agency that are more stringent than the standards prescribed by the Secretary of Commerce if the more stringent standards — (1) contain at least the applicable standards made compulsory and binding by the Secretary; and (2) are otherwise consistent with policies and guidelines issued under Section 3543 of Title 44 U.S.C. Section 302 also requires that the Secretary of Commerce promulgate any standard under the section not later than six months after the submission of the proposed standard to the Secretary by NIST, as provided under Section 20 of the National Institute of Standards and Technology Act (15 U.S.C. 278g–3).

Section 303 of the Act amends Section 20 of the National Institute of Standards and Technology Act (15 U.S.C. 278g–3), to require NIST to:

(1) Have the mission of developing standards, guidelines, and associated methods and techniques for information systems;

(2) Develop standards and guidelines, including minimum requirements, for information systems other than national security systems (as defined in Section 3542(b)(2) of Title 44,

United States Code) that are used or operated by an agency or by a contractor of an agency or other organization on behalf of an agency, other than national security systems (as defined in Section 3542(b)(2) of Title 44, United States Code); and

(3) Develop standards and guidelines, including minimum requirements, for providing adequate information security for all agency operations and assets; such standards and guidelines do not apply to national security systems.

Section 303 requires the standards and guidelines to include, among other things:

(1) Standards to be used by all agencies to categorize all information and information systems collected or maintained by or on behalf of each agency, based on the objectives of providing appropriate levels of information security according to a range of risk levels;

(2) Guidelines recommending the types of information and information systems to be included in each such category;

(3) Minimum information-security requirements for information and information systems in each category; and

(4) A definition of and guidelines concerning the detection and handling of information-security incidents.

To the maximum extent practicable, NIST is required, by Section 303 of the Act, to:

(1) Ensure that its security standards and guidelines do not require the use or procurement of specific products, including any specific hardware or software;

(2) Ensure that such standards and guidelines provide for sufficient flexibility to permit alternative solutions to provide equivalent levels of protection for identified information-security risks; and

(3) Use flexible, performance-based standards and guidelines that permit the use of off-the-shelf commercially developed information-security products.

Among other requirements of Section 303 of the Act, NIST is required to:

(1) Submit standards developed to the Secretary of Commerce for promulgation under Section 11331 of Title 40, United States Code, along with recommendations as to the extent to which these standards should be made compulsory and binding;

(2) Provide technical assistance to agencies, upon request, regarding complying with the standards and guidelines, detecting and handling information-security incidents, and information-security policies, procedures, and practices;

(3) Conduct research, as needed, to determine the nature and extent of information-security vulnerabilities and techniques for providing cost-effective information security;

(4) Develop and periodically revise performance indicators and measures for agency information-security policies and practices;

(5) Evaluate private-sector information-security policies and practices and commercially available information technologies to assess the potential application by agencies to strengthen information security;

(6) Assist the private sector, upon request, in using and applying the results of activities under this section;

(7) Evaluate security policies and practices developed for national security systems to assess the potential for application by agencies to strengthen information security; and

(8) Periodically assess the effectiveness of standards and guidelines developed under this section and undertake revisions, as appropriate.

2.2 Health Information Technology for Economic and Clinical Health (HITECH) Act

The Health Information Technology for Economic and Clinical Health (HITECH) Act of 2009 is an example of sector-specific legislation that provides for the encryption of information using NIST standards. The HITECH Act was enacted, as Title XIII of the American Recovery and Reinvestment Act of 2009, to promote the adoption and meaningful use of health information technology. Subtitle D of the HITECH Act addresses the privacy and security concerns associated with the electronic transmission of health information, in part, through several provisions that strengthen the civil and criminal enforcement of the rules enacted by the Health Insurance Portability and Accountability Act (HIPAA) of 1996[1]. The HITECH Act mandates the notification of a breach of unsecured protected health information (PHI), but provided that breaches do not have to be reported if the data involved is rendered unreadable via encryption[2].

2.3 Federal Information Systems Modernization Act of 2014

The Federal Information Systems Modernization Act of 2014 moves some of the Office of Management and Budget (OMB) responsibilities mandated by the Federal Information Security Management Act of 2002 from the Director of the Office of Management and Budget to the Secretary for Homeland Security. Paragraph 3553 requires the Secretary for Homeland Security to:

(1) Coordinate the development of standards and guidelines by NIST (under Section 20 of the National Institute of Standards and Technology Act (15 U.S.C. 278g-3)) with agencies and offices operating or exercising control of national security systems (including the National Security Agency) to assure, to the maximum extent feasible, that such standards and guidelines are complementary with standards and guidelines developed for national security systems;

---

[1] https://www.gpo.gov/fdsys/pkg/PLAW-104publ191.

[2] Data encryption, however, must be validated for compliance with NIST Federal Information Processing Standard (FIPS) 140-2, according to the Interim Final Rule that further spelled out breach notification requirements. This HHS guidance is also to be used to render identifiable health information unusable, unreadable, or indecipherable for purposes of the temporary breach notification requirements that apply to vendors of Personal Health Records (PHRs), the requirements for which are to be administered by the Federal Trade Commission (which in turn issued proposed regulations on April 16, 2009, addressing consumer notices for breaches of electronic health information by PHRs). The HHS guidance provides two methods of securing information for the purposes of the HITECH Act: destruction and encryption. Destruction may secure information that was found in either paper form or in electronic media. In order to satisfy the destruction method, the paper or other hard-copy media must be shredded or destroyed such that the PHI cannot be read or otherwise reconstructed. Electronic media must be cleared, purged, or destroyed in accordance with the specifications set forth in NIST SP 800-88. (See 74 Fed. Reg. at 19010.)

(2) Coordinate Government-wide efforts on information security policies and practices, including consultation with the Chief Information Officers Council (established under Section 3603 of the Act) and the Director of NIST;

(3) Develop and oversee the implementation of binding operational directives for agencies to implement the policies, principles, standards, and guidelines developed by the Department of Homeland Security (DHS), and consider any applicable standards or guidelines developed by NIST and issued by the Secretary of Commerce under Section 11331 of Title 40;

(4) Consult with the Director of NIST regarding any binding operational directive issued by DHS that implements standards and guidelines developed by NIST; and

(5) Ensure that the binding operational directives do not conflict with the standards and guidelines issued under Section 11331 of Title 40.

Paragraph 3553 of the Act also provides that nothing in the subchapter is to be construed as authorizing the Secretary for Homeland Security to direct the Secretary of Commerce in the development and promulgation of standards and guidelines under Section 11331 of Title 40; and that nothing in this subchapter, (Section 11331 of Title 40), or Section 20 of the National Standards and Technology Act (15 U.S.C. 278g-3) may be construed as affecting the authority of the President, the Office of Management and Budget or the Director thereof, the National Institute of Standards and Technology, or the head of any agency, with respect to the authorized use or disclosure of information, including information related to the protection of personal privacy under Title 5 or Title 44 U.S.C.

2.4 Cybersecurity Enhancement Act of 2014

The Cybersecurity Enhancement Act of 2014 extends NIST's security standards activity to include direct support to the private sector. The security standards' responsibility extension includes cryptographic standards. This extension is significant in that it specifically authorizes cybersecurity support for organizations outside the U.S. Federal government.

Specifically, the Act's *Title I: Public-Private Collaboration on Cybersecurity* - (Sec. 101) amends the National Institute of Standards and Technology Act to permit the Secretary of Commerce, acting through the Director of NIST, to facilitate and support the development of a voluntary, consensus-based, industry-led set of standards and procedures to cost-effectively reduce cyber risks to a critical infrastructure. The Act requires the NIST Director, in carrying out such activities, to:

(1) Coordinate regularly with, and incorporate the industry expertise of, relevant private-sector personnel and entities, critical infrastructure owners and operators, sector-coordinating councils, Information Sharing and Analysis Centers, and other relevant industry organizations;

(2) Consult with the heads of agencies with national security responsibilities, sector-specific agencies, state and local governments, governments of other nations, and international organizations;

(3) Identify a prioritized, flexible, repeatable, performance-based, and cost-effective approach, including information-security measures and controls, that may be voluntarily

adopted by owners and operators of a critical infrastructure to help identify, assess, and manage cyber risks; and

(4) Include methodologies to mitigate impacts on business confidentiality, protect individual privacy and civil liberties, incorporate voluntary consensus standards and industry best practices, align with international standards, and prevent duplication of regulatory processes.

However, the Act prohibits the Director from prescribing a specific solution or requiring that products or services be designed or manufactured in a particular manner, and it prohibits information provided to NIST for purposes of developing cyber-risk standards from being used by federal, state, tribal, or local agencies to regulate the activity of any entity.

The Act's Title II: Cybersecurity Research and Development - (Sec. 201) directs agencies to build upon existing programs to meet cybersecurity objectives, such as how to:

(1) Guarantee individual privacy, verify third-party software and hardware, and address insider threats;

(2) Determine the origin of messages transmitted over the Internet; and

(3) Protect information stored using cloud computing or transmitted through wireless services.

Title II also requires agencies to describe how they will focus on technologies to protect consumer privacy and enhance the security, reliability, resilience, and trustworthiness of the digital infrastructure.

The Act's Title V: Advancement of Cybersecurity Technical Standards - (Sec. 502) requires NIST to ensure the coordination of federal agencies engaged in the development of international technical standards related to information system security and instructs NIST to ensure consultation with appropriate private-sector stakeholders.

Section 503 of the Act requires consideration to be given to activities that support (in consultation with the private sector) the development of appropriate security frameworks and reference materials, and the identification of best practices, for federal agencies to use in addressing security and privacy requirements.

Section 504 of the Act requires NIST to continue a program to support the development of voluntary and cost-effective technical standards, metrology, testbeds, and conformance criteria with regard to identity management research and development.

SECTION 3: EXECUTIVE DIRECTION

This section describes directives from the Executive Office of the President (EOP) that are relevant to cryptographic standards and guidelines that are developed by NIST, or in the development of which NIST participates.

3.1 Homeland Security Presidential Directive 7 (HSPD-7): Critical Infrastructure Identification, Prioritization, and Protection

HSPD-7 establishes a national policy for federal departments and agencies to identify and prioritize United States critical infrastructure and key resources and to protect them from terrorist attacks. The Directive directs the Department of Commerce, in coordination with the Department for Homeland Security, to work with the private sector, research, academic, and government organizations to improve technology for cyber systems and promote other critical infrastructure efforts, including using its authority under the Defense Production Act[3] to assure the timely availability of industrial products, materials, and services to meet homeland security requirements.

3.2 HSPD-12: Policies for a Common Identification Standard for Federal Employees and Contractors

This directive mandates the development of a federal standard for secure and reliable forms of identification. HSPD-12 directs the Secretary of Commerce to promulgate, in accordance with applicable laws, a federal standard for secure and reliable forms of identification in consultation with the Secretary of State, the Secretary of Defense, the Attorney General, the Secretary of Homeland Security, the Director of the Office of Management and Budget (OMB), and the Director of the Office of Science and Technology Policy. The Secretary of Commerce is directed to periodically review the Standard and update the Standard, as appropriate, in consultation with the affected agencies. For purposes of this directive, "Secure and reliable forms of identification" means identification that:

(a) Is issued, based on sound criteria for verifying an individual employee's identity;

(b) Is strongly resistant to identity fraud, tampering, counterfeiting, and terrorist exploitation;

(c) Can be rapidly authenticated electronically; and

(d) Is issued only by providers whose reliability has been established by an official accreditation process.

The Standard to be developed is directed to include graduated criteria, from least secure to most secure, to ensure flexibility in selecting the appropriate level of security for each application.

---

[3] https://www.fema.gov/media-library-data/1438002689366-c84ffcf6e8476f44e0921a70a4556f88/Defense_Production_Act_2014.pdf

3.3 Executive Order 13636: Improving Critical Infrastructure Cybersecurity

Section 7 of Executive Order 13636, titled "Baseline Framework to Reduce Cyber Risk to Critical Infrastructure," requires the Secretary of Commerce to direct the Director of NIST to lead the development of a framework to reduce cyber risks to critical infrastructures (the *Cybersecurity Framework*). The *Cybersecurity Framework* was required to:

- Include a set of standards, methodologies, procedures, and processes that align policy, business, and technological approaches to address cyber risks;

- Incorporate voluntary consensus standards and industry best practices to the fullest extent possible;

- Be consistent with voluntary international standards when such international standards will advance the objectives of this order; and

- Meet the requirements of the National Institute of Standards and Technology Act, as amended (15 U.S.C. 271 et seq.), the National Technology Transfer and Advancement Act of 1995 (Public Law 104-113), and OMB Circular A-119, as revised.

The *Cybersecurity Framework* was required to:

- Provide a prioritized, flexible, repeatable, performance-based, and cost-effective approach, including information security measures and controls;

- Help owners and operators of critical infrastructures identify, assess, and manage cyber risk;

- Focus on identifying cross-sector security standards and guidelines applicable to the critical infrastructure;

- Identify areas for improvement that should be addressed through future collaboration with particular sectors and standards-developing organizations;

- In order to enable technical innovation and account for organizational differences, to provide guidance that is technology neutral and that enables critical infrastructure sectors to benefit from a competitive market for products and services that meet the standards, methodologies, procedures, and processes developed to address cyber risks; and

- Include guidance for measuring the performance of an entity in implementing the *Cybersecurity Framework*.

The *Cybersecurity Framework* was also required to include methodologies to identify and mitigate impacts of the *Cybersecurity Framework* and associated information-security measures or controls on business confidentiality, and to protect individual privacy and civil liberties.

In developing the *Cybersecurity Framework*, NIST was directed to engage in an open public review and comment process. The Director is also required to consult with the Secretary for Homeland Security, the National Security Agency, Sector-Specific agencies and other interested agencies, including OMB, owners and operators of critical infrastructure, and other stakeholders.

3.4 OMB Circular A-119: Federal Participation in the Development and Use of Voluntary Consensus Standards and in Conformity Assessment Activities

OMB Circular A-119 establishes policies on the Federal use and development of voluntary consensus standards and on conformity assessment activities. Public Law 104-113, the "National Technology Transfer and Advancement Act of 1995," codified existing policies in A-119, established reporting requirements, and authorized the National Institute of Standards and Technology to coordinate conformity assessment activities of the agencies. OMB is issuing this revision of the Circular in order to:

- Make the terminology of the Circular consistent with the National Technology Transfer and Advancement Act of 1995,

- Issue guidance to the agencies on making their reports to OMB,

- Direct the Secretary of Commerce to issue policy guidance for conformity assessment, and

- Make changes for clarity.

3.5 OMB Circular A-130: Managing Information as a Strategic Resource

Office of Management and Budget Circular A-130[4] establishes general policy for the planning, budgeting, governance, acquisition, and management of Federal information, personnel, equipment, funds, IT resources and supporting infrastructure and services. The appendices to this Circular also include responsibilities for protecting Federal information resources and managing personally identifiable information (PII). The requirements of this Circular apply to the information resources management activities of all agencies of the Executive Branch of the Federal Government. The requirements of Circular A-130 apply to management activities concerning all information resources in any medium (unless otherwise noted), including paper and electronic information. When an agency acts as a service provider, the ultimate responsibility for compliance with applicable requirements of this Circular is not shifted (to the service provider). Agencies are required to describe the responsibilities of service providers in relevant agreements with the service providers. Agencies are not required to apply this Circular to national security systems (defined in 44 U.S.C. § 3552[5]), but are encouraged to do so where appropriate. For national security systems, agencies shall follow applicable statutes, executive orders, directives, and internal agency policies.

Unlike most other cybersecurity-related directives and mandates, Circular A-130 does impose specific requirements for encryption and digital signatures. The following material identifies particularly salient requirements associated with cryptography and the underlying risk management determinations. Within each subsection below, paragraph numbers associated with lists are preserved from the Circular in order to facilitate reference.

---

[4] Although this Circular touches on many specific information resources management issues such as privacy, confidentiality, information quality, dissemination, and statistical policy, those topics are covered more fully in other Office of Management and Budget (OMB) policies, which are available on the OMB website. Agencies shall implement the policies in this Circular and those in other OMB policy guidance in a mutually consistent fashion.

[5] https://www.gpo.gov/fdsys/pkg/USCODE-2014-title44/html/USCODE-2014-title44-chap35-subchapII-sec3552.htm

3.5.1   Privacy And Information Security Provisions

Section 5, "Policy," subparagraph f, "Privacy and Information Security," subparagraph 2),
"Information Security," requires agencies to provide proper safeguards to:

a) Ensure that the CIO designates a senior agency information security officer to develop
and maintain an agency-wide information security program in accordance with the
Federal Information Security Modernization Act of 2014;

b) Protect information in a manner commensurate with the risk that would result from
unauthorized access, use, disclosure, disruption, modification, or destruction of such
information; and

c) Implement security policies issued by OMB, as well as requirements issued by the
Department of Commerce, the Department of Homeland Security (DHS), the General
Services Administration (GSA), and the Office of Personnel Management (OPM). This
includes applying the standards and guidelines contained in the NIST FIPS, NIST SPs
(e.g., 800 series guidelines), and where appropriate and directed by OMB, NIST
Interagency or Internal Reports (NISTIRs).[6]

3.5.2   Electronic Signature Provisions

Section 5, "Policy," subparagraph g, "Electronic Signatures," subparagraph 3), "Information
Security," requires agencies to:

1) Allow individuals or entities that deal with the agencies the option to submit
information or transact with the agency electronically, when practicable, and for agencies
to maintain records electronically, when practicable. Electronic records and their related
electronic signatures are not to be denied legal effect, validity, or enforceability merely
because they are in electronic form;

2) Promote the use of electronic contract formation, signatures, and recordkeeping in
private commerce by establishing legal equivalence between: contracts written on paper
and contracts in electronic form; pen-and-ink signatures and electronic signatures; and
other legally required written documents (termed "records") and the same information in
electronic form; and

3) Develop and implement processes to support use of digital signatures, a form of
electronic signature, for employees and contractors.

3.5.3   Government-wide Responsibilities

The following provisions are directed by Section 6, "Government-wide Responsibilities."

---

[6] NISTIRs describe research of a technical nature of interest to a specialized audience; NIST's cybersecurity
NISTIRs are available at http://csrc.nist.gov/publications/PubsNISTIRs.html.

a. Department of Commerce

The Secretary of Commerce shall:

1) Develop and issue standards and guidelines for the security and privacy of information in Federal information systems and systems which create, collect, Federal Government; process, store, transmit, disseminate, or dispose of information on behalf of the Federal Government; [7]

2) Provide OMB and the agencies with scientific and technical advisory services relating to the development and use of IT; [8]

3) Conduct studies and evaluations concerning telecommunications technology, and the improvement, expansion, testing, operation, and use of Federal telecommunications systems, and advise the Director of OMB and appropriate agencies of the recommendations that result from such studies;

4) Develop, in consultation with the Secretary of State and the Director of OMB, plans, policies, and programs relating to international telecommunications issues affecting Federal information activities;

5) Identify needs for standardization of telecommunications and information processing technology, and develop standards, in consultation with the Secretary of Defense and the Administrator of General Services, to ensure efficient application of such technology; [9]

6) Ensure that the Federal Government is represented in the development of national and international (in consultation with the Secretary of State) IT standards, and advise the Director of OMB on such activities; [10]

7) Evaluate new information technologies to assess their security vulnerabilities, with technical assistance from the Department of Defense (DOD) and DHS;

9) Lead the development of a Cybersecurity Framework to reduce cyber risks to critical infrastructure pursuant to Executive Order 13636, Improving Critical Infrastructure Cybersecurity.

3.5.4 General Requirements for Protecting and Managing Federal Information Resources

Appendix I, "Responsibilities for Protecting and Managing Federal Information Resources," under Section 3, "General Requirements," directs that:

---

[7] National Institute of Standards and Technologies (NIST) Act, 15 U.S.C. § 278g-3.

[8] Pursuant to the NIST Act (15 U.S.C. § 278g-3).

[9] Pursuant to the NIST Act, 15 U.S.C. §§ 272(b), 278g-3, and OMB A-119, Federal Participation in the Development and Use of Voluntary Consensus Standards and in Conformity Assessment Activities.

[10] Pursuant to NIST Act, 15 U.S.C. §§ 272(b), 273, 278g–3 and OMB A-119, Federal Participation in the Development and Use of Voluntary Consensus Standards and in Conformity Assessment Activities.

a. Agencies shall implement an agency-wide risk management process that frames, assesses, responds to, and monitors information security and privacy risk on an ongoing basis across the three organizational tiers (i.e., organization level, mission or business process level, and information system level).[11]

b. [Omitted from this publication as being out of scope.]

c. Agencies that share PII shall require, as appropriate, other agencies and entities with which they share PII to maintain the PII in an information system with a particular NIST FIPS Publication 199 confidentiality impact level, as determined by the agency sharing the PII.

d. Agencies that share PII with other agencies or entities shall impose, where appropriate, conditions (including the selection and implementation of particular security and privacy controls) that govern the creation, collection, use, processing, storage, maintenance, dissemination, disclosure, and disposal of the PII through written agreements, including contracts, data use agreements, information exchange agreements, and memoranda of understanding.

e. Agencies shall protect Controlled Unclassified Information (CUI) and shall apply NIST FIPS and NIST (800-series) SPs[12], as appropriate. This includes limiting the disclosure of proprietary information to that which is legally authorized, and impose appropriate conditions on use where a continuing obligation to ensure the confidentiality of the information exists.

f. Agencies shall ensure compliance with all applicable statutory, regulatory, and policy requirements and develop and maintain effective information security and privacy programs. This includes using privacy impact assessments and other tools to manage privacy risks.

g. Agencies shall implement policies issued by OMB, as well as requirements issued by the Department of Commerce, DHS, GSA, and OPM. This includes applying the standards and guidelines contained in NIST FIPS, NIST (800-series) SPs, and, where appropriate and directed by OMB, NISTIRs.

3.5.5 Specific Requirements for Protecting and Managing Federal Information Resources

Appendix I, "Responsibilities for Protecting and Managing Federal Information Resources," under Section 4, "Specific Requirements," directs:

a. Security Categorization

---

[11] NIST SP 800-39, *Managing Information Security Risk: Organization, Mission, and Information System View*, provides additional information on risk management processes and strategies.
[12] NIST's FIPS and SP 800-series publications are available at http://csrc.nist.gov/publications/PubsFIPS.html and http://csrc.nist.gov/publications/PubsSPs.html, respectively.

Agencies shall:

1) Identify authorization boundaries for information systems in accordance with NIST SPs 800-18 and 800-37; and

2) Categorize information and information systems, in accordance with FIPS Publication 199 and NIST SP 800-60, considering potential adverse security and privacy impacts to organizational operations and assets, individuals, other organizations, and the Nation.

c. Plans, Controls, and Assessments

Agencies shall:

5) Employ a process to select and implement security controls for information systems and the environments in which those systems operate[13] that satisfies the minimum information security requirements in FIPS Publication 200 and security control baselines in NIST SP 800-53, tailored as appropriate;

6) Employ a process to select and implement privacy controls for information systems and programs that satisfies applicable privacy requirements in OMB guidance, including, but not limited to, Appendix I to this Circular and OMB Circular A-108, Federal Agency Responsibilities for Review, Reporting, and Publication under the Privacy Act;

7) Implement information system security using sound systems security engineering principles, concepts, methods, practices, and techniques;

8) Develop and maintain security plans for information systems to document which security controls have been selected and how those controls have been implemented that satisfies the minimum information security requirements in FIPS Publication 200 and security control baselines in NIST SP 800-53, tailored as appropriate.[14]

10) Deploy effective security controls to provide Federal employees and contractors with multifactor authentication, digital signature, and encryption capabilities that provide assurance of identity and are interoperable Government-wide and accepted across all Executive Branch agencies;

---

[13] The environment of operation includes the physical surroundings in which an information system processes, stores, and transmits information. Agencies should take the environment into account when selecting, implementing, documenting, and assessing security controls.

[14] Agencies must conduct tailoring activities in accordance with OMB policy.

11) Adhere to Government-wide requirements in the deployment and use of identity credentials used by employees and contractors accessing Federal facilities;[15]

12) Designate common controls in order to provide cost-effective security and privacy[16] capabilities that can be inherited by multiple agency information systems or programs;

13) Conduct and document assessments of all selected and implemented security and privacy controls to determine whether security and privacy controls are implemented correctly, operating as intended, and sufficient to ensure compliance with applicable requirements and to manage security and privacy risks;

14) Conduct and document security and privacy control assessments prior to the operation of an information system, and periodically thereafter, consistent with the frequency defined in the agency information security continuous monitoring (ISCM) and privacy continuous monitoring (PCM) strategies and the agency risk tolerance.

i. Specific Safeguarding Measures to Reinforce the Protection of Federal Information and Information Systems[17]

Agencies shall:

4) Isolate sensitive or critical information resources (e.g., information systems, system components, applications, databases, and information) into separate security domains with appropriate levels of protection based on the sensitivity or criticality of those resources;

8) Prohibit the use of unsupported information systems and system components, and ensure that systems and components that cannot be appropriately protected or secured are given a high priority for upgrade or replacement;[18]

---

[15] NIST SP 800-116, *A Recommendation for the Use of PIV Credentials in Physical Access Control Systems (PACS)*, provides additional information on the use of PIV Credentials, the Government-wide standard identity credential, in physical access control systems. Physical access controls systems, which include, for example, servers, databases, workstations and network appliances in either shared or isolated networks, are considered information systems.

[16] When common controls protect multiple agency information systems of differing impact levels, the controls shall be implemented at the highest impact level among the systems. If such controls cannot be implemented at the highest impact level of the information systems, agencies shall factor this situation into their assessments of risk and take appropriate risk mitigation actions (e.g., adding security controls, changing assigned values of security control parameters, implementing compensating controls, changing certain aspects of mission or business processes, or separating the higher impact system into its own domain where it can be afforded appropriate levels of protection).

[17] NIST SP 800-53, *Security and Privacy Controls for Federal Information Systems and Organizations*, provides information on additional security safeguarding measures.

11) Require use of multifactor authentication for employees and contractors in accordance with Government-wide identity management standards;[19]

12) Develop and implement processes to support use of digital signatures for employees and contractors;

13) Ensure that all public key infrastructure (PKI) certificates used by an agency and issued in accordance with Federal PKI policy validate to the Federal PKI trust anchor when being used for user signing, encrypting purposes, authentication and authorization;[20]

14) Encrypt all FIPS 199 moderate-impact and high-impact information at rest and in transit, unless encrypting such information is technically infeasible or would demonstrably affect the ability of agencies to carry out their respective missions, functions, or operations; and the risk of not encrypting is accepted by the authorizing official and approved by the agency CIO, in consultation with the SAOP (as appropriate);[21]

15) Implement the current encryption algorithms and validated cryptographic modules in accordance with NIST standards and guidelines;

16) Ensure that only individuals or processes acting on behalf of individuals with legitimate need for access have the ability to decrypt sensitive information;

17) Implement data-level protection and access controls to ensure the security of and access to Federal information; and

---

[18] Includes hardware, software, or firmware components no longer supported by developers, vendors, or manufacturers through the availability of software patches, firmware updates, replacement parts, and maintenance contracts. NIST SP 800-53, *Security and Privacy Controls for Federal Information Systems and Organizations*, provides additional guidance on unsupported software components.

[19] Pursuant to Homeland Security Presidential Directive 12, *Policy for a Common Identification Standard for Federal Employees and Contractors*, NIST FIPS 201 describes the initial Government-wide identity management standard for employees and contractors as a smartcard form factor (the PIV card). With the emergence of a newer generation of computing devices and in particular with mobile devices, the use of PIV cards has evolved technically to include other form factors that can be deployed directly with mobile devices as specified in NIST SP 800-157. The PIV credential associated with this alternative is called a Derived PIV Credential. Derived PIV Credentials are based on the general concept of derived credentials in NIST SP 800-63. Issuing a Derived PIV credential to PIV card holders does not require repeating identity proofing and vetting processes. The user simply proves possession and control of a valid PIV Card to receive a Derived PIV Credential.

[20] The trust anchor refers to the Federal PKI root certificate operated by the Federal PKI Management Authority. This root certificate is the trusted source of all Federal PKI certificates. For additional information, refer to https://www.idmanagement.gov and Federal PKI policy.

[21] The encryption of organizational information when in transit over a network and when at rest in storage devices ensures that such information is persistently protected and promotes a defense-in-depth security strategy.

18) Ensure that all Federal systems and services identified in the Domain Name System are protected with Domain Name System Security (DNSSEC) and that all systems are capable of validating DNSSEC protected information.[22]

m. Encryption

When the assessed risk indicates the need, agencies must encrypt Federal information at rest and in transit unless otherwise protected by alternative physical and logical safeguards implemented at multiple layers, including networks, systems, applications, and data. Encrypting information at rest and in transit helps to protect the confidentiality and integrity of such information by making it less susceptible to unauthorized disclosure or modification. Agencies must apply encryption requirements to Federal information categorized as either moderate or high impact in accordance with FIPS Publication 199 unless encrypting such information is technically unfeasible or would demonstrably affect their ability to carry out their respective mission, functions, or operations. In situations where the use of encryption is technically infeasible, for example, due to an aging legacy system, agencies must initiate the appropriate system or system component upgrade or replacement actions at the earliest opportunity to be able to accommodate such safeguarding technologies. Authorizing officials who choose to operate information systems without the use of required encryption technologies must carefully assess the risk in doing so, and they must receive written approval for the exception from the agency CIO, in consultation with the SAOP (as appropriate). Only FIPS-validated cryptography is approved for use in Federal information systems covered by this policy.

n. Digital Signatures

Digital signatures can mitigate a variety of security vulnerabilities by providing authentication and non-repudiation capabilities, and ensuring the integrity of Federal information whether such information is used in day-to-day operations or archived for future use. Additionally, digital signatures can help agencies streamline mission or business processes and transition manual processes to more automated processes to include, for example, online transactions. Because of the advantages provided by this technology, OMB expects agencies to implement digital signature capabilities in accordance with Federal PKI policy, and NIST standards and guidelines. For employees and contractors, agencies must require the use of the digital signature capability of Personal Identity Verification (PIV) credentials. For individuals that fall outside the scope of PIV applicability, agencies should leverage approved Federal PKI credentials when using digital signatures.

3.5.6 NIST Documents Cited By Circular A-130

Circular A-130 cites the following NIST documents as references:

---

[22] DNSSEC is a critical component of the Internet infrastructure. DNSSEC enables clients to cryptographically verify that each such translation is provided by a server with the authority to do so, and that the translation response from the server was not modified before reaching the client.

8) National Institute of Standards and Technology Federal Information Processing Standards Publication 199, Standards for Security Categorization of Federal Information and Information Systems.

9) National Institute of Standards and Technology Federal Information Processing Standards Publication 200, Minimum Security Requirements for Federal Information and Information Systems.

10) National Institute of Standards and Technology Federal Information Processing Standards Publication 201, Personal Identity Verification of Federal Employees and Contractors.

11) National Institute of Standards and Technology Special Publication 800-18, Guide for Developing Security Plans for Federal Information Systems.

12) National Institute of Standards and Technology Special Publication 800-30, Guide for Conducting Risk Assessments.

13) National Institute of Standards and Technology Special Publication 800-37, Guide for Applying the Risk Management Framework to Federal Information Systems: A Security Life Cycle Approach.

14) National Institute of Standards and Technology Special Publication 800-39, Managing Information Security Risk: Organization, Mission, and Information System View.

15) National Institute of Standards and Technology Special Publication 800-47, Security Guide for Interconnecting Information Technology Systems.

16) National Institute of Standards and Technology Special Publication 800-53, Security and Privacy Controls for Federal Information Systems and Organizations.

17) National Institute of Standards and Technology Special Publication 800-53A, Guide for Assessing the Security Controls in Federal Information Systems and Organizations: Building Effective Security Assessment Plans.

18) National Institute of Standards and Technology Special Publication 800-59, Guideline for Identifying an Information System as a National Security System.

19) National Institute of Standards and Technology Special Publication 800-60, Guide for Mapping Types of Information and Information Systems to Security Categories.

20) National Institute of Standards and Technology Special Publication 800-63, Electronic Authentication Guideline.

21) National Institute of Standards and Technology Special Publication 800-73, Interfaces for Personal Identity Verification.

22) National Institute of Standards and Technology Special Publication 800-76, Biometric Specifications for Personal Identity Verification.

23) National Institute of Standards and Technology Special Publication 800-78, Cryptographic Algorithms and Key Sizes for Personal Identity Verification.

24) National Institute of Standards and Technology Special Publication 800-79, Guidelines for the Authorization of Personal Identity Verification Card Issuers (PCI) and Derived PIV Credential Issuers (DPCI).

25) National Institute of Standards and Technology Special Publication 800-116, Guidelines for the Use of PIV Credentials in Physical Access Control Systems (PACS).

26) National Institute of Standards and Technology Special Publication 800-122, Guide to Protecting the Confidentiality of Personally Identifiable Information (PII).

27) National Institute of Standards and Technology Special Publication 800-137, Information Security Continuous Monitoring for Federal Information Systems and Organizations.

28) National Institute of Standards and Technology Special Publication 800-157, Guidelines for Derived Personal Identity Verification Credentials.

29) National Institute of Standards and Technology Special Publication 800-161, Supply Chain Risk Management Practices for Federal Information Systems and Organizations.

30) National Institute of Standards and Technology Special Publication 800-162, Guide to Attribute Based Access Control (ABAC) Definition and Considerations.

31) National Institute of Standards and Technology Special Publication 800-171, Protecting Controlled Unclassified Information in Nonfederal Information Systems and Organizations.

32) National Institute of Standards and Technology Framework for Improving Critical Infrastructure Cybersecurity.

33) National Institute of Standards and Technology Supplemental Guidance on Ongoing Authorization: Transitioning to Near Real-Time Risk Management.

3.6 OMB Memorandum M-06-16: Protection of Sensitive Agency Information

OMB Memorandum M-06-16 notes that NIST provided a checklist for the protection of remote information. The intent of implementing the checklist is to compensate for the lack of physical security controls when information is removed from, or accessed from outside the agency location. In addition to using the NIST checklist, OMB M-06-16 recommended that all departments and agencies encrypt all data on mobile computers/devices that carry agency data unless the data is determined to be non-sensitive, in writing, by a Deputy Secretary or an individual that he/she may designate in writing; and allow remote access only with two-factor authentication where one of the factors is provided by a device separate from the computer gaining access.

3.7 OMB Memorandum M-06-18, Acquisition of Products and Services for Implementation of HSPD-12

OMB Memorandum M-06-18 provides updated direction for the acquisition of products and services for the implementation of Homeland Security Presidential Directive-12 (HSPD-12), *Policy for a Common Identification Standard for Federal Employees and Contractors*, and also provides the status of implementation efforts.

HSPD-12 notes that both NIST and the General Services Administration (GSA) have established evaluation programs for the testing and evaluation of specific products and services needed for the implementation of HSPD-12, and that NIST has established the NIST Personal Identity Verification Program (NPIVP) to test and validate Personal Identity Verification (PIV) components and sub-systems required by Federal Information Processing Standard (FIPS) 201. At the time that the Memorandum was signed, an NPIVP validation program provided for the testing and validation of PIV card applications and PIV middleware for conformance to FIPS 201 and the interface specifications of NIST SP 800-73, *Interfaces for Personal Identity Verification*. NIST was also noted as having published derived test requirements as NIST SP 800-85A, *PIV Card Application and Middleware Test Guidelines*. All of the tests under NPIVP are handled by third-party test laboratories that are now designated as interim NPIVP Test Facilities.

FIPS 140-2, *Security Requirements for Cryptographic Modules*[23], requires the testing and validation of the cryptographic modules of PIV cards and other products performing cryptographic functions. This testing is performed by the accredited third-party facilities designated to perform NPIVP testing.

3.8 OMB Memorandum M-07-16, Safeguarding Against and Responding to the Breach of Personally Identifiable Information

OMB Memorandum M-07-16 requires agencies to develop and implement a breach[24] notification policy within 120 days from the OMB Memorandum's having been signed. The Memorandum specifically recommends using encryption, strong authentication procedures, and other security controls to make information unusable by unauthorized individuals. The attachments to this memorandum outline the framework within which agencies must develop this breach notification policy, while ensuring that proper safeguards are in place to protect the information. Elements of the framework include requirements to:

---

[23] Note that implementation of FIPS 140-2 by the Cryptographic Module Validation Program is accomplished in accordance with the *Implementation Guidance for FIPS PUB 140-2 and the Cryptographic Module Validation Program*, which is periodically updated to list additional clarification/guidance relating to FIPS 140-2.

[24] For the purposes of this policy, the term "breach" is used to include the loss of control, compromise, unauthorized disclosure, unauthorized acquisition, unauthorized access, or any similar term referring to situations where persons other than authorized users or for an other than authorized purpose have access or potential access to personally identifiable information, whether physical or electronic.

a. <u>Assign an impact level to all information and information systems</u>. Agencies must follow the processes outlined in FIPS 199, *Standards for Security Categorization of Federal Information and Information Systems*, to categorize all information and information systems according to the standard's three levels of impact (i.e., low, moderate, and high). Agencies should generally consider categorizing sensitive, personally identifiable information (and information systems within which such information resides) as moderate or high impact.

b. <u>Implement minimum security requirements and controls</u>. For each of the impact levels identified above, agencies must implement the minimum security requirements and minimum (baseline) security controls set forth in FIPS 200, *Minimum Security Requirements for Federal Information and Information Systems,* and NIST Special Publication 800-53, *Recommended Security Controls for Federal Information Systems*[25], respectively.

c. <u>Certify and accredit information systems</u>. Agencies must certify and accredit (C&A) all information systems supporting the operations and assets of the agency, including those provided or managed by another agency, contractor, or other source. The specific procedures for conducting C&A are set out in NIST Special Publication 800-37, *Guide for the Security Certification and Accreditation of Federal Information Systems,*[26] and include guidance for the continuous monitoring of certain security controls. Agencies' continuous monitoring should assess a subset of the management, operational, and technical controls used to safeguard such information (*e.g.*, Privacy Impact Assessments).

The Memorandum's requirements include 1) encryption using only NIST-certified cryptographic modules[27] for all data on mobile computers/devices carrying agency data, unless the data is determined to not be sensitive, in writing, by a Deputy Secretary[28] or a senior-level individual he/she may designate in writing; and 2) allowing remote access only with two-factor authentication where one of the factors is provided by a device separate from the computer gaining access.

3.9 OMB Memorandum M-08-23: Securing the Federal Government's Domain Name System Infrastructure (DNS)

OMB Memorandum M-08-23 required the Federal Government to deploy Domain Name System Security Extensions (DNSSEC) to the top-level .gov domain by January 2009. The top-level .gov domain includes the registrar, registry, and DNS server operations. This policy requires that the top-level .gov domain will be DNSSEC-signed, and processes to enable secure delegated sub-domains will be developed. Signing the top-level .gov domain is a critical procedure necessary for broad deployment of DNSSEC, increases the utility of DNSSEC, and simplifies lower-level deployment by agencies.

The Memorandum also required agencies to develop plans of action and milestones for the deployment of DNSSEC to all applicable information systems. Appropriate DNSSEC capabilities were required to be deployed and operational by December 2009. The plans were to follow recommendations in NIST SP 800-81, *Secure Domain Name System (DNS) Deployment Guide*, and

---

[25] The current Revision 4 of SP 800-53 is titled *Security and Privacy Controls for Federal Information Systems and Organizations*.

[26] Since reissued as SP 800-37 Revision 1, *Guide for Applying the Risk Management Framework for Federal Information Systems: A Security Life Cycle Approach.* Note that certification is no longer required and the term *C&A* is now obsolete.

[27] See NIST's website at http://csrc.nist.gov/cryptval/ for a discussion of the validated encryption modules.

[28] Non-cabinet agencies should consult the equivalent of a Deputy Secretary.

address the particular requirements described in NIST SP 800-53r1[29], *Recommended Security Controls for Federal Information Systems*. The plans were also to report agencies' current levels of compliance with the current DNSSEC requirements of NIST SP 800-53r1, and document plans of action and milestones that assume the scope of the requirement to operate DNSSEC signed zones. SP 800-53's control SC-20 was required to be expanded to cover all FISMA information systems (including low-impact systems) in its revision 3. The plans were to ensure that all agency .gov domains were DNSSEC-signed by December 2009.

3.10 OMB Memorandum M-11-33: FY 2011 Reporting Instructions for the Federal Information Security Management Act and Agency Privacy Management

OMB Memorandum M-11-33 includes "Frequently Asked Questions on Reporting for the Federal Information Security Management Act and Agency Privacy Management." The following frequently asked questions included with the Memorandum are relevant to cryptographic applications:

Must the Department of Defense (DOD) and the Office of the Director of National Intelligence (ODNI) follow OMB policy and NIST guidelines?

Yes, for non-national security systems, DOD and ODNI are to incorporate OMB policy and NIST guidelines into their internal policies.

For national security systems, the Joint Task Force Transformation Initiative (JTFTI) Interagency Working Group, with representatives from the Civil, Defense and Intelligence Communities (IC) started an on-going effort in FY2009 to produce a unified information-security framework for the Federal Government. Under this effort, DOD, ODNI and NIST jointly issued the following publications:

- NIST SP 800-37, Revision 1, *Guide for Applying the Risk Management Framework to Federal Information Systems,* February 2010.

- NIST SP 800-38A, *Recommendation for Block Cipher Modes of Operation,* December 2001.

- NIST SP 800-39, *Managing Information Security Risk: Organization, Mission, and Information System View,* March 2011.

- NIST SP 800-53 Revision 3[30], *Recommended Security Controls for Federal Information Systems and Organizations,* August 2009.

Because these guidelines are jointly issued, DOD and ODNI policies for national security systems should incorporate these guidelines.

Is use of National Institute of Standards and Technology (NIST) publications required?

Yes. For non-national security programs and information systems, agencies must follow NIST standards and guidelines unless otherwise stated by OMB. For legacy information systems, agencies are expected to be in compliance with NIST standards and guidelines

---

[29] The Memorandum referenced an earlier version, Revision 1. The publication has been updated. The current revision is Revision 4.

[30] The Memorandum referenced an earlier version, Revision 3. The publication has been updated. The current revision is Revision 4.

within one year of the publication date unless otherwise directed by OMB. The one-year compliance date for revisions to NIST publications applies only to the new and/or updated material in the publications. For information systems under development or for legacy systems undergoing significant changes, agencies are expected to be in compliance with the NIST publications immediately upon deployment of the information system.

Are NIST guidelines flexible?

Yes. While agencies are required to follow NIST standards and guidelines in accordance with OMB policy, there is flexibility within NIST's guidelines (specifically in the 800-series) in how agencies apply them. However, NIST Federal Information Processing Standards (FIPS) publications are mandatory. Unless specified by additional implementing policy by OMB, NIST guidelines generally allow agencies latitude in their application. Consequently, the application of NIST guidelines by agencies can result in different security solutions that are equally acceptable and compliant with the guidelines.

FISMA, OMB policy, and NIST standards and guidelines require agency security programs to be risk-based. Who is responsible for deciding the acceptable level of risk (e.g., the CIO, program officials and system owners, or the IG)? Are the IGs' independent evaluations also to be risk-based? What if they disagree?

The agency head ultimately is responsible for deciding the acceptable level of risk for their agency. System owners, program officials, and CIOs provide input for this decision. Such decisions must reflect policies from OMB and standards and guidelines from NIST (particularly FIPS 199, *Standards for Security Categorization of Federal Information and Information Systems,* and FIPS 200, *Minimum Security Requirements for Federal Information and Information Security,* as well as SP 800-39, *Managing Information Security Risk*). An information system' s Authorizing Official takes responsibility for accepting any residual risk, thus they are held accountable for managing the security for that system.

IG evaluations are intended to independently assess that the agency is applying a risk-based approach to their information security programs and the information systems that support the conduct of agency missions and business functions. For example, when reviewing the assessment in support of an individual security authorization, the IG would generally assess whether: 1) the assessment was performed in the manner prescribed in NIST guidelines and agency policy, 2) controls are being implemented as stated in any planning documentation, and 3) continuous monitoring is adequate given the system impact level of the system and information.

Are there security requirements specific for mobile devices (e.g. smartphones and tablets)?

All existing Federal requirements for data protection and remote access are applicable to mobile devices. For example, the security requirements in OMB Circular A-130, FIPS 140-2, *Security Requirements for Cryptographic Modules,* FIPS 199, *Standards for Security Categorization of Federal Information and Information Systems,* and FIPS 200, *Minimum Security Requirements for Federal Information and Information Systems,* apply (including appropriate security controls specified in SP 800-53). Agencies should specify security requirements during the acquisition process and ensure that procurements capture the requirements of the Federal Acquisition Regulation[31] (e.g., 52.225-5, Trade Agreements), OMB policy (e.g., M-06-16 and M-07-16), and NIST standards and guidelines. Additional guidance regarding the use and management of mobile devices will be developed, as appropriate.

3.11 OMB Memorandum M-16-03, Fiscal Year 2015-2016 Guidance on Federal Information Security and Privacy Management Requirements

OMB Memorandum M-16-03 notes that, in early FY 2015, OMB and the National Security Council (NSC) staff created a quarterly cybersecurity assessment organized according to the functions in the NIST *Framework for Improving Critical Infrastructure Cybersecurity (Identify, Protect, Detect, Respond, and Recover)* and associated outcomes to comprehensively assess agency cybersecurity performance. The assessment builds on the existing foundation of FISMA metrics and the Cybersecurity Cross Agency Priority (CAP)[32] goals, and is reviewed by agency senior leadership. Moving forward, the Memorandum states that this assessment will be the cornerstone initiative for how OMB measures Federal agency cybersecurity performance.

---

[31] Federal Acquisition Regulation, https://www.acquisition.gov/?q=browsefar [accessed 8/8/2016].
[32] *GPRA Modernization Act of 2010, Public Law 111-352,* https://www.performance.gov/cap-goals-list [accessed 8/8/2016].

SECTION 4: ORGANIZATIONAL POLICIES

Every federal organization has (or should have) policies that address the information that they collect or create, including an Information Management Policy and an Information Security Policy. Organizations utilizing cryptography should also have a Key Management Policy.

4.1 Information Management Policy

An organization's Information Management Policy specifies what information is to be collected or created, and how it is to be managed. An organization's management establishes this policy using industry standards of good practices, legal requirements regarding the organization's information, and organizational goals that must be achieved using the information that the organization will be collecting and creating.

An Information Management Policy typically identifies management roles and responsibilities and establishes the authorization required for people performing these information-management duties. It also specifies what information is to be considered sensitive and how it is to be protected. In particular, this policy specifies what categories of information need to be protected against unauthorized disclosure, modification or destruction. These specifications form the foundation for an Information Security Policy and dictate the levels of confidentiality, integrity, availability, and source-authentication protections that must be provided for differing categories of sensitive information (see SP 800-130, *A Framework for Designing Cryptographic Key Management Systems*).

Section 4.1 of SP 800-152, *A Profile for U.S. Federal Cryptographic Key Management Systems*, provides requirements for the content of an Information Management Policy for federal agencies.

4.2 Information Security Policy

An organization's Information Security Policy is created to support and enforce portions of the organization's Information Management Policy by specifying in more detail what information is to be protected from anticipated threats and how that protection is to be attained. The rules for collecting, protecting, and distributing sensitive information in both paper and electronic form are specified in this policy. The inputs to the Information Security Policy include, but are not limited to, the Information Management Policy specifications, the potential threats to the security of the organization's information, and the risks involved with the unauthorized disclosure, modification, and destruction or loss of the information.

The outputs of the Information Security Policy include the information sensitivity levels (e.g., low, medium, or high) assigned to various categories of information and the high-level rules for protecting the information (see SP 800-130, *A Framework for Designing Cryptographic Key Management Systems*).

Section 4.2 of SP 800-152 provides requirements for the content of an Information Security Policy for federal agencies.

4.3 Key Management Policies

Each organization that manages cryptographic systems that are intended to protect sensitive information should base the management of the keys used in those systems on an organizational policy statement. The Key Management Policy includes descriptions of the authorization and protection objectives and constraints that apply to the generation, distribution, accounting, storage, use, recovery and destruction of cryptographic keying material, and the cryptographic services to be provided (e.g., message authentication, digital signature, and encryption).

Further information and requirements for Key Management Policies is provided in Section 3 of SP 800-57 Part 2, *Recommendation for Key Management, Part 2: Best Practices for Key Management Organization.*

Key-Management Systems manage the cryptographic keys used to protect an organization's sensitive information. Federal organizations may operate their own key-management systems, or may contract for key-management services. Information and requirements on the key management systems that manage cryptographic keys is provided in SP 800-152.

SECTION 5: RISK MANAGEMENT PROCESS

SP 800-37, *Guide for Applying the Risk Management Framework to Federal Information Systems: A Security Lifecycle Approach*, provides guidelines for applying the Risk Management Framework to federal information systems to include conducting the activities of security categorization,[33] security control selection and implementation, security control assessment, information system authorization,[34] and security control monitoring. The guidelines have been developed:

- To ensure that managing information-system-related security risks is consistent with the organization's mission/business objectives and overall risk strategy established by the senior leadership through the risk executive (function);

- To ensure that information security requirements, including the necessary security controls, are integrated into the organization's enterprise architecture and system development life cycle processes;

- To support consistent, well-informed, and ongoing security authorization decisions (through continuous monitoring), transparency of security and risk management-related information, and reciprocity;[35] and

- To achieve more secure information and information systems within the federal government through the implementation of appropriate risk mitigation strategies.

When dealing with cryptographic functions, the tasks involved in applying the Risk Management Framework to information systems focus more on:

- The categorization of information and information systems and the selection of security controls than on the implementation of security controls,

- The assessment of security control effectiveness,

- The authorization of the information system, and

- The ongoing monitoring of security controls and the security state of the information system.

---

[33] FIPS 199 provides security-categorization guidance for non-national security systems. CNSS Instruction 1253 provides similar guidance for national security systems.

[34] System *authorization* is the official management decision given by a senior organizational official to authorize the operation of an information system and to explicitly accept the risk to organizational operations and assets, individuals, other organizations, and the Nation, based on the implementation of an agreed-upon set of security controls.

[35] *Reciprocity* is the mutual agreement among participating organizations to accept each other's security assessments in order to reuse information-system resources and/or to accept each other's assessed security posture in order to share information. Reciprocity is best achieved by promoting the concept of transparency (i.e., making sufficient evidence regarding the security state of an information system available, so that an authorizing official from another organization can use that evidence to make credible, risk-based decisions regarding the operation and use of that system or the information it processes, stores, or transmits).

5.1 Categorization of Information and Information Systems

Categorization of information and information systems requires the organization to:

- Categorize the information system and document the results of the security categorization in the security plan as described in FIPS 199; SP 800-30, SP 800-39, SP 800-59, SP 800-60, and CNSS Instruction 1253;

- Describe the information system (including the system boundary) and document the description in the security plan; and

- Register the information system with appropriate organizational program/management offices.

5.2 Selection of Security Controls

The selection of security controls involves the following steps:

- Identify the security controls that are provided by the organization as common controls for organizational information systems and document the controls in a security plan (or equivalent document) in accordance with FIPS 199, FIPS 200, SP 800-30, SP 800-53 and CNSS Instruction 1253;

- Select the security controls for the information system and document the controls in the security plan as described in FIPS 199, FIPS 200; SP 800-30, SP 800-53 and CNSS Instruction 1253;

- Develop a strategy for the continuous monitoring of security-control effectiveness and any proposed or actual changes to the information system and its environment of operation as described in SP 800-30, SP 800-39, SP 800-53, SP 800-53A, SP 800-137 and CNSS Instruction 1253; and

- Review and approve the security plan in accordance with SP 800-30, SP 800-53 and CNSS Instruction 1253.

APPENDIX A: REFERENCES

1. Public Law 104-113, *National Technology Transfer and Advancement Act of 1995*, 104th Congress, March 7, 1996. https://www.gpo.gov/fdsys/pkg/PLAW-104publ113/content-detail.html [accessed 8/8/2016].

2. Public Law 107-347, *E-Government Act of 2002*, 107th Congress, December 17, 2002. https://www.gpo.gov/fdsys/pkg/PLAW-107publ347/pdf/PLAW-107publ347.pdf [accessed 8/8/2016].

3. Public Law 111-5, *American Recovery and Reinvestment Act of 2009*, "Health Information Technology for Economic and Clinical Health Act (HITECH Act)," 111th Congress, February 17, 2009. https://www.gpo.gov/fdsys/pkg/PLAW-111publ5/pdf/PLAW-111publ5.pdf [accessed 8/8/2016].

4. Public Law 111-352, *GPRA Modernization Act of 2010*, 111th Congress, January 4, 2011. https://www.gpo.gov/fdsys/pkg/PLAW-111publ352/pdf/PLAW-111publ352.pdf [accessed 8/8/2016].

5. Public Law 113-274, *Cybersecurity Enhancement Act of 2014*, 113th Congress, December 18, 2014. https://www.gpo.gov/fdsys/pkg/PLAW-113publ274/content-detail.html [accessed 8/8/2016].

6. Public Law 113-283, *Federal Information Systems Modernization Act of 2014*, 113th Congress, December 18, 2014. https://www.congress.gov/113/plaws/publ283/PLAW-113publ283.pdf [accessed 8/8/2016].

7. *National Institute of Standards and Technology*, Title 15 U.S. Code, Sec. 271 *et seq.*, 2014 ed. https://www.gpo.gov/fdsys/granule/USCODE-2014-title15/USCODE-2014-title15-chap7 [accessed 8/8/2016].

8. *Computer standards program*, Title 15 U.S. Code, Sec. 278g-3, 2014 ed. https://www.gpo.gov/fdsys/granule/USCODE-2014-title15/USCODE-2014-title15-chap7-sec278g-3 [accessed 8/8/2016].

9. *Responsibilities for Federal information systems standards*, Title 40 U.S. Code, Sec. 11331, 2014 ed. https://www.gpo.gov/fdsys/granule/USCODE-2014-title40/USCODE-2014-title40-subtitleIII-chap113-subchapIII-sec11331 [accessed 8/8/2016].

10. Executive Office of the President, The White House, *Critical Infrastructure Identification, Prioritization, and Protection*, Homeland Security Presidential Directive 7 (HSPD-7), December 17, 2003. https://www.dhs.gov/homeland-security-presidential-directive-7 [accessed 8/8/2016].

11. Executive Office of the President, The White House, *Policies for a Common Identification Standard for Federal Employees and Contractors*, Homeland Security Presidential Directive 12 (HSPD-12), August 27, 2004. https://www.dhs.gov/homeland-security-presidential-directive-12 [accessed 8/8/2016].

12. Executive Office of the President, The White House, *Improving Critical Infrastructure Cybersecurity*, Executive Order 13636, February 12, 2013. https://federalregister.gov/a/2013-03915 [accessed 8/8/2016].

13. Executive Office of the President, Office of Management and Budget, *Federal Participation in the Development and Use of Voluntary Consensus Standards and in Conformity Assessment Activities*, OMB Circular Number A-119, Revised, February 10, 1998. https://www.whitehouse.gov/omb/circulars_a119/ [accessed 8/8/2016].

14. Executive Office of the President, Office of Management and Budget, *Managing Information As a Strategic Resource,* OMB Circular Number A-130, Revised, July 28, 2016. https://www.whitehouse.gov/sites/default/files/omb/assets/OMB/circulars/a130/a130revised.pdf [accessed 8/8/2016].

15. Executive Office of the President, Office of Management and Budget, *Protection of Sensitive Agency Information*, OMB Memorandum M-06-16, June 23, 2006. https://www.whitehouse.gov/sites/default/files/omb/memoranda/fy2006/m06-16.pdf [accessed 8/8/2016].

16. Executive Office of the President, Office of Management and Budget, *Acquisition of Products and Services for Implementation of HSPD-12*, OMB Memorandum M-06-18, June 30, 2006. https://www.whitehouse.gov/sites/default/files/omb/assets/omb/memoranda/fy2006/m06-18.pdf [accessed 8/8/2016].

17. Executive Office of the President, Office of Management and Budget, *Safeguarding Against and Responding to the Breach of Personally Identifiable Information*, OMB Memorandum M-07-16, May 27, 2007. https://www.whitehouse.gov/sites/default/files/omb/memoranda/fy2007/m07-16.pdf [accessed 8/8/2016].

18. Executive Office of the President, Office of Management and Budget, *Securing the Federal Government's Domain Name System Infrastruc*ture, OMB Memorandum M-08-23, August 22, 2008. https://www.whitehouse.gov/sites/default/files/omb/memoranda/fy2008/m08-23.pdf [accessed 8/8/2016].

19. Executive Office of the President, Office of Management and Budget, *FY 2011 Reporting Instructions for the Federal Information Security Management Act and Agency Privacy Management*, OMB Memorandum M-11-33, September 14, 2011. https://www.whitehouse.gov/sites/default/files/omb/memoranda/2011/m11-33.pdf [accessed 8/8/2016].

20. Executive Office of the President, Office of Management and Budget, *Guidance on Federal Information Security and Privacy Management Requirements*, OMB Memorandum M-16-03, October 30, 2015. https://www.whitehouse.gov/sites/default/files/omb/memoranda/2016/m-16-03.pdf [accessed 8/8/2016].

21. Federal Information Processing Standard 140-2 (FIPS 140-2), *Security Requirements for Cryptographic Modules*, National Institute of Standards and Technology, May 2001 (updated 12/3/2002, Change Notice 2). http://csrc.nist.gov/publications/fips/fips140-2/fips1402.pdf [accessed 8/8/2016].

22. Federal Information Processing Standard 199 (FIPS 199), *Standards for Security Categorization of Federal Information and Information Systems*, National Institute of

Standards and Technology, February 2004.
http://csrc.nist.gov/publications/fips/fips199/FIPS-PUB-199-final.pdf [accessed 8/8/2016].

23. Federal Information Processing Standard 200 (FIPS 200), *Minimum Security Requirements for Federal Information and Information Systems*, National Institute of Standards and Technology, March 2006. http://csrc.nist.gov/publications/fips/fips200/FIPS-200-final-march.pdf [accessed 8/8/2016].

24. Federal Information Processing Standard 201-2 (FIPS 201-2), *Personal Identity Verification (PIV) of Federal Employees and Contractors*, National Institute of Standards and Technology, April 2013. http://dx.doi.org/10.6028/NIST.FIPS.201-2.

25. National Institute of Standards and Technology, *Framework for Improving Critical Infrastructure Cybersecurity,* Version 1.0, February 12, 2015. http://www.nist.gov/cyberframework/upload/cybersecurity-framework-021214.pdf [accessed 8/8/2016].

26. National Institute of Standards and Technology, *Guide for Developing Security Plans for Federal Information Systems*, NIST Special Publication 800-18 Rev. 1, February 2006. http://dx.doi.org/10.6028/NIST.SP.800-18r1.

27. National Institute of Standards and Technology, *Guide for Conducting Risk Assessments*, NIST Special Publication 800-30 Rev. 1, September 2012. http://dx.doi.org/10.6028/NIST.SP.800-30r1.

28. National Institute of Standards and Technology, *Guide for Applying the Risk Management Framework to Federal Information Systems: A Security Life Cycle Approach*, NIST Special Publication 800-37 Rev. 1, February 2010 (updated 6/5/2014). http://dx.doi.org/10.6028/NIST.SP.800-37r1.

29. National Institute of Standards and Technology, *Recommendation for Block Cipher Modes of Operation: Methods and Techniques*, NIST Special Publication 800-38A, December 2001. http://dx.doi.org/10.6028/NIST.SP.800-38A.

30. National Institute of Standards and Technology, *Managing Information Security Risk: Organization, Mission, and Information System View*, NIST Special Publication 800-39, March 2011. http://dx.doi.org/10.6028/NIST.SP.800-39.

31. National Institute of Standards and Technology, *Security Guide for Interconnecting Information Technology Systems*, NIST Special Publication 800-47, August 2002. http://dx.doi.org/10.6028/NIST.SP.800-47.

32. National Institute of Standards and Technology, *Security and Privacy Controls for Federal Information Systems and Organizations*, NIST Special Publication 800-53 Rev. 4, April 2013 (updated 1/22/2015). http://dx.doi.org/10.6028/NIST.SP.800-53r4.

33. National Institute of Standards and Technology, *Assessing Security and Privacy Controls in Federal Information Systems and Organizations: Building Effective Assessment Plans*, NIST Special Publication 800-53A, December 2014 (updated 12/18/2014). http://dx.doi.org/10.6028/NIST.SP.800-53Ar4.

34. National Institute of Standards and Technology, *Recommendation for Key Management, Part 2: Best Practices for Key Management Organization*, NIST Special Publication 800-57 Part 2, August 2005. http://dx.doi.org/10.6028/NIST.SP.800-57p2.

35. National Institute of Standards and Technology, *Guideline for Identifying an Information System as a National Security System*, NIST Special Publication 800-59, August 2003. http://dx.doi.org/10.6028/NIST.SP.800-59.

36. National Institute of Standards and Technology, *Guide for Mapping Types of Information and Information Systems to Security Categories*, NIST Special Publication 800-60 Rev. 1 (2 vols.), August 2008. http://dx.doi.org/10.6028/NIST.SP.800-60v1r1; http://dx.doi.org/10.6028/NIST.SP.800-60v2r1.

37. National Institute of Standards and Technology, *Electronic Authentication Guideline*, NIST Special Publication 800-63-2, August 2013. http://dx.doi.org/10.6028/NIST.SP.800-63-2.

38. National Institute of Standards and Technology, *Interfaces for Personal Identity Verification*, NIST Special Publication 800-73-4, May 2015 (updated 2/8/2016). http://dx.doi.org/10.6028/NIST.SP.800-73-4.

39. National Institute of Standards and Technology, *Biometric Specifications for Personal Identity Verification*, NIST Special Publication 800-76-2, July 2013. http://dx.doi.org/10.6028/NIST.SP.800-76-2.

40. National Institute of Standards and Technology, *Cryptographic Algorithms and Key Sizes for Personal Identity Verification*, NIST Special Publication 800-78-4, May 2015. http://dx.doi.org/10.6028/NIST.SP.800-78-4.

41. National Institute of Standards and Technology, *Guidelines for the Authorization of Personal Identity Verification Card Issuers (PCI) and Derived PIV Credential Issuers (DPCI)*, NIST Special Publication 800-79-2, July 2015. http://dx.doi.org/10.6028/NIST.SP.800-79-2.

42. National Institute of Standards and Technology, *Secure Domain Name System (DNS) Deployment Guide*, NIST Special Publication 800-81-2, September 2013. http://dx.doi.org/10.6028/NIST.SP.800-81-2.

43. National Institute of Standards and Technology, *PIV Card Application and Middleware Interface Test Guidelines (SP800-73-4 Compliance)*, NIST Special Publication 800-85A-4, April 2016. http://dx.doi.org/10.6028/NIST.SP.800-85A-4.

44. National Institute of Standards and Technology, *Guidelines for Media Sanitization*, NIST Special Publication 800-88 Rev. 1, December 2014. http://dx.doi.org/10.6028/NIST.SP.800-88r1.

45. National Institute of Standards and Technology, *A Recommendation for the Use of PIV Credentials in Physical Access Control Systems (PACS)*, NIST Special Publication 800-116, November 2008. http://dx.doi.org/10.6028/NIST.SP.800-116.

46. National Institute of Standards and Technology, *Guide to Protecting the Confidentiality of Personally Identifiable Information (PII)*, NIST Special Publication 800-122, April 2010. http://dx.doi.org/10.6028/NIST.SP.800-122.

47. National Institute of Standards and Technology, *A Framework for Designing Cryptographic Key Management Systems*, NIST Special Publication 800-130, August 2013. http://dx.doi.org/10.6028/NIST.SP.800-130.

48. National Institute of Standards and Technology, *Information Security Continuous Monitoring (ISCM) for Federal Information Systems and Organizations*, NIST Special Publication 800-137, September 2011. http://dx.doi.org/10.6028/NIST.SP.800-137.

49. National Institute of Standards and Technology, *A Profile for U. S. Federal Cryptographic Key Management Systems (CKMS)*, NIST Special Publication 800-152, October 2015. http://dx.doi.org/10.6028/NIST.SP.800-152.

50. National Institute of Standards and Technology, *Guidelines for Derived Personal Identity Verification (PIV) Credentials*, NIST Special Publication 800-157, December 2014. http://dx.doi.org/10.6028/NIST.SP.800-157.

51. National Institute of Standards and Technology, *Supply Chain Risk Management Practices for Federal Information Systems and Organizations*, NIST Special Publication 800-161, April 2015. http://dx.doi.org/10.6028/NIST.SP.800-161.

52. National Institute of Standards and Technology, *Guide to Attribute Based Access Control (ABAC) Definition and Considerations*, NIST Special Publication 800-162, January 2014. http://dx.doi.org/10.6028/NIST.SP.800-162.

53. National Institute of Standards and Technology, *Protecting Controlled Unclassified Information in Nonfederal Information Systems and Organizations*, NIST Special Publication 800-171, June 2015 (updated 1/14/2016). http://dx.doi.org/10.6028/NIST.SP.800-171.

54. National Institute of Standards and Technology, *Guideline for Using Cryptographic Standards in the Federal Government: Cryptographic Mechanisms*, NIST Special Publication 800-175B, August 2016. http://dx.doi.org/10.6028/NIST.SP.800-175B.

55. Committee on National Security Systems (CNSS), *Security Categorization and Control Selection for National Security Systems*, CNSS Instruction 1253, March 27, 2014. Available at: https://www.cnss.gov/CNSS/issuances/Instructions.cfm [accessed 8/8/2016].

56. National Institute of Standards and Technology, and the Communications Security Establishment Canada, *Implementation Guidance for FIPS PUB 140-2 and the Cryptographic Module Validation Program,* CMVP, March 28, 2003, Last Update June 17, 2016. http://csrc.nist.gov/groups/STM/cmvp/documents/fips140-2/FIPS1402IG.pdf [accessed 8/8/2016].

57. National Institute of Standards and Technology, *Supplemental Guidance on Ongoing Authorization: Transitioning to Near Real-Time Risk Management*, June 2014. http://csrc.nist.gov/publications/nistpubs/800-37-rev1/nist_oa_guidance.pdf [accessed 8/8/2016].

NIST Special Publication 800-175B

Guideline for Using Cryptographic Standards in the Federal Government:
Cryptographic Mechanisms

Elaine Barker

This publication is available free of charge from:
http://dx.doi.org/10.6028/NIST.SP.800-175B

COMPUTER SECURITY

NIST Special Publication 800-175B

Guideline for Using Cryptographic Standards in the Federal Government:

Cryptographic Mechanisms

Elaine Barker
Computer Security Division
Information Technology Laboratory

This publication is available free of charge from:
http://dx.doi.org/10.6028/NIST.SP.800-175B

August 2016

U.S. Department of Commerce
Penny Pritzker, Secretary

National Institute of Standards and Technology
Willie May, Under Secretary of Commerce for Standards and Technology and Director

Authority

This publication has been developed by NIST in accordance with its statutory responsibilities under the Federal Information Security Modernization Act (FISMA) of 2014, 44 U.S.C. § 3551 *et seq.*, Public Law (P.L.) 113-283. NIST is responsible for developing information security standards and guidelines, including minimum requirements for federal information systems, but such standards and guidelines shall not apply to national security systems without the express approval of appropriate federal officials exercising policy authority over such systems. This guideline is consistent with the requirements of the Office of Management and Budget (OMB) Circular A-130.

Nothing in this publication should be taken to contradict the standards and guidelines made mandatory and binding on federal agencies by the Secretary of Commerce under statutory authority. Nor should these guidelines be interpreted as altering or superseding the existing authorities of the Secretary of Commerce, Director of the OMB, or any other federal official. This publication may be used by nongovernmental organizations on a voluntary basis and is not subject to copyright in the United States. Attribution would, however, be appreciated by NIST.

National Institute of Standards and Technology Special Publication 800-175B
Natl. Inst. Stand. Technol. Spec. Publ. 800-175B, 73 pages (August 2016)
CODEN: NSPUE2

This publication is available free of charge from:
http://dx.doi.org/10.6028/NIST.SP.800-175B

Certain commercial entities, equipment, or materials may be identified in this document in order to describe an experimental procedure or concept adequately. Such identification is not intended to imply recommendation or endorsement by NIST, nor is it intended to imply that the entities, materials, or equipment are necessarily the best available for the purpose.

There may be references in this publication to other publications currently under development by NIST in accordance with its assigned statutory responsibilities. The information in this publication, including concepts and methodologies, may be used by federal agencies even before the completion of such companion publications. Thus, until each publication is completed, current requirements, guidelines, and procedures, where they exist, remain operative. For planning and transition purposes, federal agencies may wish to closely follow the development of these new publications by NIST.

Organizations are encouraged to review all draft publications during public comment periods and provide feedback to NIST. Many NIST cybersecurity publications, other than the ones noted above, are available at http://csrc.nist.gov/publications.

Comments on this publication may be submitted to:

National Institute of Standards and Technology
Attn: Computer Security Division, Information Technology Laboratory
100 Bureau Drive (Mail Stop 8930) Gaithersburg, MD 20899-8930
Email: SP800-175@nist.gov

All comments are subject to release under the Freedom of Information Act (FOIA).

Reports on Computer Systems Technology

The Information Technology Laboratory (ITL) at the National Institute of Standards and Technology (NIST) promotes the U.S. economy and public welfare by providing technical leadership for the Nation's measurement and standards infrastructure. ITL develops tests, test methods, reference data, proof of concept implementations, and technical analyses to advance the development and productive use of information technology. ITL's responsibilities include the development of management, administrative, technical, and physical standards and guidelines for the cost-effective security and privacy of other than national security-related information in federal information systems. The Special Publication 800-series reports on ITL's research, guidelines, and outreach efforts in information system security, and its collaborative activities with industry, government, and academic organizations.

Abstract

This document is intended to provide guidance to the Federal Government for using cryptography and NIST's cryptographic standards to protect sensitive, but unclassified digitized information during transmission and while in storage. The cryptographic methods and services to be used are discussed.

Keywords

asymmetric-key algorithm; authentication; confidentiality; cryptography; digital signatures; encryption; integrity; key agreement; key derivation; key management; key transport; key wrapping; message authentication codes; non-repudiation; Public Key Infrastructure (PKI); random bit generation; symmetric-key algorithm.

Acknowledgments

The author wishes to thank the authors of SP 800-21 from which this document was derived, Annabelle Lee and William C. Barker, along with those colleagues that reviewed drafts of this document and contributed to its development: Lily Chen, Shu-jen Chang, and Kerry McKay. The author also gratefully acknowledges and appreciates the many comments from the public and private sectors whose thoughtful and constructive comments improved the quality and usefulness of this publication.

Table of Contents

SECTION 1: INTRODUCTION

1.1   Overview and Purpose

In today's environment of increasingly open and interconnected systems and networks and the use of mobile devices, network and data security are essential for the optimum safe use of this information technology. Cryptographic techniques should be considered for the protection of data that is sensitive, has a high value, or is vulnerable to unauthorized disclosure or undetected modification during transmission or while in storage.

Cryptography is a branch of mathematics that is based on the transformation of data and can be used to provide several security services: confidentiality, data integrity authentication, and source authentication, and also to support non-repudiation.

- *Confidentiality* is the property whereby sensitive information is not disclosed to unauthorized entities. Confidentiality can be provided by a cryptographic process called *encryption*.

- *Data integrity* is a property whereby data has not been altered in an unauthorized manner since it was created, transmitted or stored. The process of determining the integrity of the data is called *data integrity authentication*.

- *Source authentication* is a process that provides assurance of the source of information to a receiving entity; source authentication can also be considered as identity authentication (i.e., providing assurance of an entity's identity). A special case of source authentication is called *non-repudiation*, whereby support for assurance of the source of the information is provided to a third party.

This document is one part in a series of documents intended to provide guidance to the Federal Government for using cryptography to protect its sensitive, but unclassified digitized information during transmission and while in storage; hereafter, the shortened term "sensitive" will be used to refer to this class of information. Other sectors are invited to use this guidance on a voluntary basis. The following are the initial publications in the Special Publication (SP) 800-175 subseries. Additional documents may be provided in the future.

- SP 800-175A provides guidance on the determination of requirements for using cryptography. It includes the laws and regulations for the protection of the Federal Government's sensitive information, guidance for the conduct of risk assessments to determine what needs to be protected and how best to protect that information, and a discussion of the required security-related documents (e.g., various policy and practice documents).

- SP 800-175B (this document) discusses the cryptographic methods and services available for the protection of the Federal Government's sensitive information and provides an overview of NIST's cryptographic standards.

1.2   Audience

This document is intended for federal employees and others who are responsible for providing and using cryptographic services to meet identified security requirements. This document might be used by:

- Program managers responsible for selecting and integrating cryptographic mechanisms into a system;

- A technical specialist requested to select one or more cryptographic methods/techniques to meet a specified requirement;

- A procurement specialist developing a solicitation for a system, network or service that will require cryptographic methods to perform security functionality; and

- Users of cryptographic services.

The goal is to provide these individuals with sufficient information to allow them to make informed decisions about the cryptographic methods that will meet their specific needs to protect the confidentiality and integrity of data that is transmitted and/or stored in a system or network, as well as to obtain assurance of its authenticity.

This document is not intended to provide information on the federal procurement process or to provide a technical discussion on the mathematics of cryptography and cryptographic algorithms.

1.3   Scope

This document limits its discussion of cryptographic methods to those that conform to Federal Information Processing Standards (FIPS) and NIST Special Publications (SPs), which are collectively discussed as NIST "standards" in this document. While the Federal Government is required to use these standards, when applicable, industry and national and international standards bodies have also adopted these cryptographic methods.

This document provides information on selecting and using cryptography in new or existing systems.

1.4   Background

The use of cryptography relies upon two basic components: an *algorithm* and a *key*. The algorithm is a mathematical function, and the key is a parameter used during the cryptographic process. The algorithm and key are used together to apply cryptographic protection to data (e.g., to encrypt the data or to generate a digital signature) and to remove or check the protection (e.g., to decrypt the encrypted data or to verify the digital signature). The security of the cryptographic protection relies on the secrecy of the key. Security should not rely on the secrecy of the algorithm, as the algorithm specification may be publicly available.

In order to use a cryptographic algorithm, cryptographic keys must be "in place," i.e., keys must be established for and/or between parties that intend to use cryptography. Keys may be established either manually (e.g., via a trusted courier) or using an automated method. However, when an automated method is used, authentication is required for the participating entities that relies on an established trust infrastructure, such as a Public Key Infrastructure (PKI) or on a manually distributed authentication key.

In general, keys used for one purpose (e.g., the generation of digital signatures) must not be used for another purpose (e.g., for key establishment) because the use of the same key for two different cryptographic processes may weaken the security provided by one or both of the processes. See Section 5.2 in SP 800-57, Part 1[1] for further information.

1.5 Terms and Definitions

The following terms and definitions are used in this document. In general, the definitions are drawn from FIPS and NIST Special Publications.

Algorithm	A clearly specified mathematical process for computation; a set of rules that, if followed, will give a prescribed result.
Approved	FIPS-Approved and/or NIST-recommended. An algorithm or technique that is either 1) specified in a FIPS or NIST recommendation, or 2) specified elsewhere and adopted by reference in a FIPS or NIST Recommendation.
Asymmetric-key algorithm	See *public-key algorithm*.
Authentication	A process that provides assurance of the source and integrity of information that is communicated or stored.
Bit string	An ordered sequence of 0's and 1's.
Block cipher algorithm	A family of functions and their inverse functions that is parameterized by cryptographic keys; the functions map bit strings of a fixed length to bit strings of the same length.
Certificate (or public key certificate)	A set of data that uniquely identifies an entity, contains the entity's public key and possibly other information, and is digitally signed by a trusted party, thereby binding the public key to the entity identified in the certificate. Additional information in the certificate could specify how the key is used and the validity period of the certificate.
Certificate Revocation List (CRL)	A list of revoked but unexpired certificates issued by a Certification Authority.

---

[1] SP 800-57 Part 1, *Recommendation for Key Management: General Guideline.*

3

Certification Authority (CA)	The entity in a public key infrastructure (PKI) that is responsible for issuing certificates and exacting compliance to a PKI policy.
Ciphertext	Data in its encrypted form.
Compromise	The unauthorized disclosure, modification, substitution or use of sensitive data (e.g., keying material and other security-related information).
Confidentiality	The property that sensitive information is not disclosed to unauthorized entities.
Cross certify	The establishment of a trust relationship between two Certification Authorities (CAs) through the signing of each other's public key in a certificate referred to as a "cross-certificate."
Cryptographic algorithm	A well-defined computational procedure that takes variable inputs, including a cryptographic key (if applicable), and produces an output.
Cryptographic boundary	An explicitly defined continuous perimeter that establishes the physical bounds of a cryptographic module and contains all the hardware, software and/or firmware components of a cryptographic module.
Cryptographic checksum	A mathematical value created using a cryptographic algorithm that is assigned to data and later used to test the data to verify that the data has not changed.
Cryptographic hash function	A function that maps a bit string of arbitrary length to a fixed-length bit string. **Approved** hash functions satisfy the following properties: 1. (One-way) It is computationally infeasible to find any input that maps to any pre-specified output, and 2. (Collision resistant) It is computationally infeasible to find any two distinct inputs that map to the same output.
Cryptographic key	A parameter used in conjunction with a cryptographic algorithm that determines its operation in such a way that an entity with knowledge of the key can reproduce or reverse the operation, while an entity without knowledge of the key cannot. Examples include: 1. The transformation of plaintext data into ciphertext data, 2. The transformation of ciphertext data into plaintext data,

4

	3. The computation of a digital signature from data, 4. The verification of a digital signature, 5. The computation of an authentication code from data, 6. The verification of an authentication code from data and a received authentication code, and 7. The computation of a shared secret that is used to derive keying material.
Cryptographic module	The set of hardware, software and/or firmware that implements **approved** security functions (including cryptographic algorithms and key generation) and is contained within a cryptographic boundary.
Cryptographic primitive	A low-level cryptographic algorithm used as a basic building block for higher-level cryptographic algorithms.
Cryptography	The discipline that embodies the principles, means and methods for providing information security, including confidentiality, data integrity, and non-repudiation.
Cryptoperiod	The time span during which a specific key is authorized for use or in which the keys for a given system may remain in effect.
Data integrity	A property whereby data has not been altered in an unauthorized manner since it was created, transmitted or stored.
Decryption	The process of changing ciphertext into plaintext using a cryptographic algorithm and key.
Digital signature	The result of a cryptographic transformation of data that, when properly implemented, provides the services of: 1. Source authentication, 2. Data integrity, and 3. Supports signer non-repudiation.
Digital Signature Algorithm (DSA)	A public-key algorithm that is used for the generation and verification of digital signatures.
Elliptic Curve Digital Signature Algorithm (ECDSA)	A digital signature algorithm that is an analog of DSA using elliptic curves.
Encryption	The process of changing plaintext into ciphertext for the purpose of security or privacy.

Entity	An individual (person), organization, device or process.
Ephemeral key pair	A short-term key pair that is generated when needed; the public key of an ephemeral key pair is not provided in a public key certificate, unlike static public keys which often are.
Function	As used in this document, used interchangeability with algorithm.
Hash function	See *cryptographic hash function*.
Hash value	The result of applying a hash function to information; also called a message digest.
Initialization Vector (IV)	A vector used in defining the starting point of a cryptographic process.
Integrity	The property that data has not been modified or deleted in an unauthorized and undetected manner.
Interoperability	The ability of one entity to communicate with another entity.
Key	See *cryptographic key*.
Key agreement	A (pair-wise) key-establishment procedure where the resultant secret keying material is a function of information contributed by two participants, so that no party can predetermine the value of the secret keying material independently from the contributions of the other party. Contrast with key-transport.
Key derivation	The process by which one or more keys are derived from either a pre-shared key, or a shared secret and other information.
Key establishment	The procedure that results in keying material that is shared among different parties.
Key management	The activities involving the handling of cryptographic keys and other related security parameters (e.g., IVs and counters) during the entire life cycle of the keys, including the generation, storage, establishment, entry and output, and destruction.
Key pair	A public key and its corresponding private key; a key pair is used with a public key (asymmetric-key) algorithm.
Key transport	A key-establishment procedure whereby one party (the sender) selects a value for the secret keying material and then securely distributes that value to another party (the receiver). Contrast with key agreement.

Key-wrapping key	A symmetric key used to provide confidentiality and integrity protection for other keys.
Keying material	The data (e.g., keys and IVs) necessary to establish and maintain cryptographic keying relationships.
Keying relationship, cryptographic	The state existing between two entities such that they share at least one cryptographic key.
Message Authentication Code (MAC)	A cryptographic checksum on data that uses a symmetric key to detect both accidental and intentional modifications of data.
Message digest	See *hash value*.
Mode of operation	An algorithm that uses a block cipher algorithm to provide a cryptographic service, such as confidentiality or authentication.
NIST standard	Federal Information Processing Standard (FIPS) or Special Publication (SP).
Non-repudiation	A service using a digital signature that is used to support a determination of whether a message was actually signed by a given entity.
Plaintext	Data that has not been encrypted.
Primitive	See *Cryptographic primitive*.
Private key	A cryptographic key, used with a public key cryptographic algorithm that is uniquely associated with an entity and is not made public. In an asymmetric (public) key cryptosystem, the private key is associated with a public key. Depending on the algorithm, the private key may be used to: 1. Compute the corresponding public key, 2. Compute a digital signature that may be verified by the corresponding public key, 3. Decrypt data that was encrypted by the corresponding public key, or 4. Compute a shared secret during a key-agreement process.
Public key	A cryptographic key used with a public-key cryptographic algorithm, that is uniquely associated with an entity and that may be made public. In an asymmetric (public) key cryptosystem, the public key is associated with a private key. The public key may be known by anyone and, depending on the

	algorithm, may be used to: 1. Verify a digital signature that is signed by the corresponding private key, 2. Encrypt data that can be decrypted by the corresponding private key, 3. Compute a shared secret during a key-agreement process.
Public key (asymmetric) cryptographic algorithm	A cryptographic algorithm that uses two related keys, a public key and a private key. The two keys have the property that determining the private key from the public key is computationally infeasible.
Public Key Infrastructure (PKI)	A framework that is established to issue, maintain and revoke public key certificates.
Relying party	An entity that relies on the certificate and the CA that issued the certificate to verify the identity of the certificate owner, and the validity of the public key, associated algorithms and any relevant parameters in the certificate, as well as the owner's possession of the corresponding private key.
RSA	A public-key algorithm that is used for key establishment and the generation and verification of digital signatures.
Secret key	A cryptographic key that is used with a symmetric (secret key) cryptographic algorithm and is not made public. The use of the term "secret" in this context does not imply a classification level, but rather implies the need to protect the key from disclosure. Compare with a private key, which is used with a public key algorithm.
Secret key (symmetric) cryptographic algorithm	See symmetric (secret key) algorithm.
Sensitive (information)	Sensitive, but unclassified information.
Security strength	A number associated with the amount of work (that is, the number of operations) that is required to break a cryptographic algorithm or system.
Shared secret	A secret value that is computed during a key-agreement transaction and is used as input to derive a key using a key-derivation method.

Signature generation	The use of a <u>digital signature algorithm</u> and a <u>private key</u> to generate a <u>digital signature</u> on data.
Signature verification	The use of a <u>digital signature</u> and a <u>public key</u> to verify a digital signature on data.
Source authentication	A process that provides assurance of the source of information.
Static key pair	A long-term <u>key pair</u> for which the <u>public key</u> is often provided in a public-key <u>certificate</u>.
Symmetric key	A single <u>cryptographic key</u> that is used with a <u>symmetric (secret key) algorithm</u>. Also called a <u>secret key</u>.
Symmetric (secret key) algorithm	A <u>cryptographic algorithm</u> that uses the same <u>secret key</u> for an operation and its complement (e.g., <u>encryption</u> and <u>decryption</u>).

1.6   Acronyms

AES	Advanced Encryption Standard; specified in <u>FIPS 197</u>.
ANS	American National Standard.
ANSI	American National Standard Institute.
ASC	Accredited Standards Committee.
CA	Certification Authority.
CBC	Cipher Block Chaining mode; specified in <u>SP 800-38A</u>.
CFB	Cipher Feedback mode; specified in <u>SP 800-38A</u>.
CKMS	Cryptographic Key Management System.
CP	Certificate Policy.
CPS	Certification Practice Statement.
CRL	Certificate Revocation List.
CTR	Counter mode; specified in <u>SP 800-38A</u>.
DES	Data Encryption Standard; originally specified in FIPS 46; now provided in <u>SP 800-67</u>.
DH	Diffie-Hellman algorithm.
DNSSEC	Domain Name System Security Extensions.
DRBG	Deterministic Random Bit Generator; specified in <u>SP 800-90A</u>.
DSA	Digital Signature Algorithm; specified in <u>FIPS 186</u>.
ECB	Electronic Codebook mode; specified in <u>SP 800-38A</u>.
ECDSA	Elliptic Curve Digital Signature Algorithm.
EMC	Electromagnetic Compatibility.
FCKMS	Federal Cryptographic Key Management System.
FIPS	Federal Information Processing Standard.
FISMA	Federal Information Security Management Act.
GCM	Galois Counter Mode; specified in <u>SP 800-38D</u>.
HMAC	Keyed-Hash Message Authentication Code; specified in <u>FIPS 198</u>.
IEC	International Electrotechnical Commission.

IEEE	Institute of Electrical and Electronics Engineers.
IETF	Internet Engineering Task Force.
EMI	Electromagnetic Interference.
INCITS	International Committee for Information Technology Standards.
IPSEC	Internet Protocol Security.
ISO	International Standards Organization.
IT	Information Technology.
MAC	Message Authentication Code.
MQV	Menezes-Qu-Vanstone algorithm; specified in SP 800-56A.
NRBG	Non-deterministic Random Bit Generator.
NIST	National Institute of Standards and Technology.
OFB	Output Feedback mode; specified in SP 800-38A.
OTAR	Over-the-Air-Rekeying.
PKI	Public Key Infrastructure.
RA	Registration Authority.
RBG	Random Bit Generator.
RFC	Request for Comment.
RSA	A public key algorithm attributed to Rivest, Shamir and Adleman.
SHA	Secure Hash Algorithm.
SP	Special Publication.
SSH	Secure Shell protocol.
TCG	Trusted Computing Group.
TDEA	Triple Data Encryption Algorithm; specified in SP 800-67.
TLS	Transport Layer Security.

1.7   Content

This document is organized into the following sections:

- Section 1 provides an introduction to the SP 800-175 series of publications and to this document in particular, and provides a glossary of terms and a list of acronyms.

- Section 2 discusses the importance of standards, as well as the national and international standards bodies concerned with cryptography.

- Section 3 introduces the **approved** algorithms used for encryption, digital signature and key-establishment, and provides discussions on security strengths and algorithm lifetime.

- Section 4 discusses the services that cryptography can provide: data confidentiality, data integrity authentication, source authentication and support for non-repudiation.

- Section 5 discusses the key management required for the use of cryptography, providing general guidance and discussions on key-management systems, key-establishment mechanisms and random bit generation.

- Section 6 discusses additional issues associated with the use of cryptography.

There is one appendix in this document:

- Appendix A lists applicable Federal Information Processing Standards, recommendations, and guidelines.

SECTION 2: STANDARDS AND GUIDELINES

2.1   Benefits of Standards

Standards define common practices, methods, and measures/metrics. Standards provide solutions that have been evaluated by experts in relevant areas, reviewed by the public and subsequently accepted by a wide community of users. By using standards, organizations can reduce costs and protect their investments in technology.

Standards provide the following benefits:

- **Interoperability.** Products developed to a specific standard may be used to provide interoperability with other products that conform to the same standard. For example, by using the same cryptographic encryption algorithm, data that was encrypted using vendor A's product may be decrypted using vendor B's product. The use of a common standards-based cryptographic algorithm is necessary, but may not be sufficient to ensure product interoperability. Other common standards, such as communications protocol standards, may also be necessary.

  By ensuring interoperability among the products of different vendors, standards permit an organization to select from various available products to find the most cost-effective solution.

- **Security.** Standards may be used to establish a common level of security. For example, most agency managers are not cryptographic security experts, and, by using an **approved** cryptographic algorithm and key length, a manager knows that the algorithm has been found to be adequate for the protection of sensitive government data and has been subjected to a significant period of public analysis and comment.

- **Quality.** Standards may be used to assure the quality of a product. Standards may:

  o Specify how a feature is to be implemented,

  o Require self-tests to ensure that the product is still functioning correctly, and

  o Require specific documentation to assure proper implementation and product-change management.

  Many NIST standards have associated conformance tests and specify the conformance requirements. The conformance tests may be administered by NIST-accredited laboratories and provide validation that the NIST standard was correctly implemented.

- **Common Form of Reference.** A NIST standard may become a common form of reference to be used in testing/evaluating a vendor's product. For example, FIPS 140[2] contains security and integrity requirements for *any* cryptographic module implementing cryptographic operations.

---

[2] FIPS 140, *Security Requirements for Cryptographic Modules*.

- **Cost Savings.** Implementations that comply with commonly accepted specifications provided by standards can save money. Without standards, users may be required to become experts in every information technology (IT) product that is being considered for procurement. Also, without standards, products may not interoperate with different products purchased by other users. This could result in a significant waste of money or in the delay of implementing IT.

2.2 Federal Information Processing Standards and Special Publications

2.2.1 The Use of FIPS and SPs

The use of a Federal Information Processing Standard (FIPS) is *mandatory* for the Federal Government whenever the type of service specified in that standard is required by a federal agency for the protection of sensitive information. For example, FIPS 197[3] contains a specific set of technical security requirements for the AES algorithm. Whenever AES is used by an agency, its implementation and use must conform to FIPS 197. A FIPS is **approved** by the Secretary of Commerce.

A NIST Special Publication (SP) is similar to a FIPS, but is not mandatory unless a particular government agency (e.g., OMB) makes it so. An SP does not need the approval of the Secretary of Commerce.

Although the requirements for the use of a FIPS and an SP are different, both types of publications have been subjected to the same review process by the federal agencies and the public. The approval process for a FIPS is more formal than that of an SP, and subsequently takes longer for the initial approval and the approval of any subsequent revisions.

When a federal agency requires the use of cryptography (e.g., for encryption), an **approved** algorithm must be used; approval is indicated by inclusion in a FIPS or SP. For example, two **approved** algorithms for encryption are AES (as specified in FIPS 197) and TDEA (as specified in SP 800-67[4]). Whenever encryption is used by a federal agency for the protection of sensitive information, either AES or TDEA must be used. Whenever AES is to be used, it must be implemented as specified in FIPS 197; whenever TDEA is to be used, it must be implemented as specified in SP 800-67. In addition to using **approved** algorithms, federal agencies are required to use only implementations of these algorithms that have been validated and are included in validated cryptographic modules (see Section 5.4.5 for further discussion).

When developing a specification or the criteria for the selection of a cryptographic mechanism or service, cryptographic algorithms specified in FIPS and SPs must be used, when available. Some guidelines may be used to specify the functions that the algorithm will perform (e.g., FIPS 199[5] or SP 800-53[6]). Other NIST standards specify the

---

[3] FIPS 197, *Advanced Encryption Standard (AES)*.

[4] SP 800-67, *Recommendation for the Triple Data Encryption Algorithm (TDEA) Block Cipher*.

[5] FIPS 199, *Standards for Security Categorization of Federal Information and Information Systems*.

[6] SP 800-53, *Security and Privacy Controls for Federal Information Systems and Organizations*.

operation and use of specific types of algorithms (e.g., AES, DSA) and the level of independent testing required for classes of security environments (e.g., FIPS 140).

Appendix A contains a list of FIPS and SPs that apply to the implementation of cryptography in the Federal Government. Note that when a FIPS is revised, its number is commonly followed by a revision number that indicates the number of times that it has been revised (e.g., "FIPS 186-4" is used to indicate the fourth revision of FIPS 186); this practice is not used in the main body of this document; the reader must refer to the latest version of the FIPS or SP that has been officially **approved** (see http://csrc.nist.gov/publications/; note that this site also contains clearly marked draft publications) .

2.2.2 FIPS Waivers

In the past, a waiver was sometimes issued by an agency to indicate that the use of a FIPS was not required by that agency. However, the Federal Information Security Management Act (FISMA) of 2002 (P.L. 107-347) eliminated previously authorized provisions for waivers from FIPS (see SP 800-175A for a discussion).

2.3 Other Standards Organizations

NIST develops standards, recommendations, and guidelines that are used by vendors who are developing security products, components, and modules. These products may be acquired and used by federal government agencies. In addition, there are other groups that develop and promulgate standards. These organizations are briefly described below.

2.3.1 American National Standards Institute (ANSI) [7]

The American National Standards Institute (ANSI) is the administrator and coordinator of the United States' private-sector voluntary standardization system. ANSI does not develop American National Standards itself; rather, it facilitates the development of standards by establishing consensus among qualified groups.

Several ANSI committees have developed standards that use cryptography, but the primary committee that has developed standards for the cryptographic algorithms themselves is Accredited Standards Committee (ASC) X9, which is a financial-industry committee[8]. Many of the standards developed within ASC X9 have been adopted within NIST standards (e.g., the Elliptic Curve Digital Signature Algorithm specified in American National Standard X9.62[9] has been adopted in FIPS 186); likewise, ASC X9 has approved the use of NIST standards via a registry of approved standards from non-ASC X9 sources (e.g., AES, as specified in FIPS 197).

A number of ASC X9 standards have also been incorporated into the standards of other standards bodies, such as the International Standards Organization (ISO) (see Section

---

[7] Further information is available at the ANSI web site: www.ansi.org.

[8] Further information is available at the ANSI X9 web site: x9.org.

[9] ANS X9.62, *Public Key Cryptography for the Financial Services Industry: The Elliptic Curve Digital Signature Algorithm (ECDSA)*.

2.3.4) via a Technical Advisory Group (TAG) called the International Committee on Information Technology Standards (INCITS). INCITS has been responsible for assuring that U.S. standards (e.g., both those developed by NIST and those developed within ASC X9) are incorporated within ISO standards.

2.3.2 Institute of Electrical and Electronics Engineers (IEEE) Standards Association [10]

IEEE is an international, professional association that is dedicated to advancing technological innovation and excellence. The technical objectives of the IEEE focus on advancing the theory and practice of electrical, electronics and computer engineering, and computer science. IEEE develops and disseminates voluntary, consensus-based industry standards involving leading-edge electro-technology. IEEE supports international standardization and encourages the development of globally acceptable standards.

The Institute of Electrical and Electronics Engineers Standards Association (IEEE-SA) is an organization within IEEE that develops global standards. It has more than one thousand active standards, some of which are related to cryptography.

IEEE P1363 [11] is the only IEEE standard that focuses on cryptography. It includes a series of standards on public-key cryptography. IEEE P1363 was developed at the same time as the ANSI public-key cryptographic standards, such as ANS X9.31 [12], X9.42 [13], X9.44 [14], X9.62 [15], and X9.63 [16], which were developed in ASC X9 (see Section 2.4.1).

- The first part of the IEEE P1363 standard was published in 2000 and revised in 2004 as IEEE P1363a [17]. It includes the basic public-key cryptography schemes, such as RSA encryption, signatures, the Digital Signature Algorithm (DSA), and key establishment using Diffie-Hellman (DH) and Menezes-Qu-Vanstone (MQV) over finite fields and elliptic curves.

- IEEE P1363.1 [18], which was published in 2008, specifies NTRU encryption and signature schemes.

---

[10] Further information is available at the IEEE-SA web site: standards.ieee.org.

[11] IEEE P1363: *Standard Specifications for Public-Key Cryptography.*

[12] ANS X9.31, *Digital Signatures Using Reversible Public Key Cryptography for the Financial Services Industry (rDSA)*, which has now been withdrawn.

[13] ANS X9.42, *Agreement of Symmetric Keys Using Discrete Logarithm Cryptography*, which has now been withdrawn.

[14] ANS X9.44, *Key Establishment Using Integer Factorization Cryptography.*

[15] ANS X9.62, *The Elliptic Curve Digital Signature Algorithm (ECDSA).*

[16] ANS X9.63, *Key Agreement and Key Transport Using Elliptic Curve Cryptography.*

[17] IEEE P1363a, *Standard Specifications for Public Key Cryptography - Amendment 1: Additional Techniques.*

[18] IEEE P1363.1, *Public-Key Cryptographic Techniques Based on Hard Problems over Lattices.*

- IEEE P1363.2[19] was also published in 2008. It specifies password-authenticated key agreement and password-authenticated key retrieval schemes.

The schemes specified in IEEE P1363.1 and P1363.2 are not included in the NIST standards.

Cryptographic schemes are used in IEEE standards for different applications. One of the more notable is the IEEE 802 LAN/MAN group of standards, which are widely used computer networking standards for both wired (Ethernet) and wireless (IEEE 802.11[20]) networks. Cryptographic algorithms are used to protect wireless communications. The CCM mode for authentication and confidentiality specified in SP 800-38C was adopted from IEEE 802.11. Other AES modes of operation (e.g., GCM, which is specified in SP 800-38D) are also used in IEEE 802 standards. IEEE 802 standards also use the SHA-1 and SHA-2 family of hash functions specified in FIPS 180 and used in HMAC, as specified in FIPS 198.

XTS, a block cipher mode of operation specified in SP 800-38E, was adopted from IEEE P1619[21] as SP 800-38E.

2.3.3 Internet Engineering Task Force (IETF)

The Internet Engineering Task Force (IETF) is an international community of network designers, operators, vendors, researchers, and technologists that work on the Internet architecture, and its techniques and protocols. An IETF official technical specification or recommendation is called a Request for Comments (RFC).

The technical work of the IETF is done in its working groups, which are organized by topic into several areas, such as routing, transport and security. In the security area, different working groups develop security mechanisms for different protocols or applications. For example,

1. The PKIX (Public-Key Infrastructure X.509) Working Group (PKIX-WG) developed technical specifications and recommendations to support a Public Key Infrastructure, based on the X.509 protocol, which is used to build a trust and authentication services infrastructure,

2. The IPSEC (Internet Protocol Security) working group developed a protocol and other technical recommendations for secure routing between network devices, and

3. The TLS (Transport Layer Security) working group has been specifying a communication protocol and technical recommendations to provide security services for communication between a server and a client, etc.

NIST-approved cryptographic algorithms, such as block cipher modes of operation, hash functions, key establishment schemes, and digital signatures are used in various IETF protocols. For example, RFC 5288 specifies the AES Galois Counter Mode (GCM) Cipher Suites for TLS, based on SP 800-38D.

---

[19] IEEE P1363.2, *Password-Based Public-Key Cryptography*.

[20] IEEE 802.11, *Wireless Local Area Networks*.

[21] IEEE P1619, *Standard for Cryptographic Protection of Data on Block-Oriented Storage Devices*.

Further information is available at the IETF web site, http://ietf.org.

2.3.4   International Organization for Standardization (ISO)[22]

ISO is a non-governmental, worldwide federation of national standards bodies. Its mission is to develop international standards that help to make industry more efficient and effective. ISO standards cover almost all aspects of technology and business, from food safety to computers, and from agriculture to healthcare. Experts from all over the world develop the standards that are required by their sector, using a consensus process.

ISO/IEC JTC 1 is a joint technical committee of the International Organization for Standardization (ISO) and the International Electrotechnical Commission (IEC). ISO/IEC JTC 1 SC 27 is the subcommittee for IT security. Working group 2 (WG2) is the group developing standards for cryptography and security mechanisms. It usually has more than twenty active projects to develop either a revision of an existing standard or a new standard. Each standard consists of multiple parts, and each part includes multiple algorithms and/or mechanisms.

The cryptographic algorithms and schemes in FIPS and SPs are usually included in ISO/IEC JTC 1 standards, along with many other algorithms submitted by other countries. The following is a list of ISO/IEC standards that include cryptographic algorithms and schemes specified in NIST standards.

1. ISO/IEC 9797-1:2011, *Information technology − Security techniques − Message Authentication Codes (MACs) -- Part 1: Mechanisms using a block cipher.*

2. ISO/IEC 9797-2:2011, *Information technology − Security techniques − Message Authentication Codes (MACs) -- Part 2: Mechanisms using a dedicated hash-function.*

3. ISO/IEC 10116:2006, *Information technology − Security techniques − Modes of operation for an n-bit block cipher.*

4. ISO/IEC 10118-3:2004, *Information technology − Security techniques − Hash-functions -- Part 3: Dedicated hash-functions.*

5. ISO/IEC 11770-3:2008, *Information technology − Security techniques − Key management -- Part 3: Mechanisms using asymmetric techniques.*

6. ISO/IEC CD 11770-6, *Information technology − Security techniques − Key management -- Part 6: Key derivation.*

7. ISO/IEC 14888-2: 2008, *Information technology − Security techniques − Digital signatures with appendix -- Part 2: Integer factorization based mechanisms.*

8. ISO/IEC CD 14888-3, *Information technology − Security techniques − Digital signatures with appendix -- Part 3: Discrete logarithm based mechanisms.*

9. ISO/IEC 18033-3:2010, *Information technology − Security techniques − Encryption algorithms − Part 3: Block ciphers.*

---

[22] Further information is available at the ISO web site, http://www.iso.org.

10. ISO/IEC 19772:2009, *Information technology – Security techniques – Authenticated encryption.*

2.3.5   Trusted Computing Group (TCG)

The Trusted Computing Group (TCG) develops and promotes a set of industry standards that build upon roots of trust. Roots of Trust (RoTs) are hardware, firmware, and software components that are inherently trusted to perform specific, vital security functions. Because misbehavior by RoTs cannot be detected, they must be secure by design. To ensure that they are reliable and resistant to tampering, RoTs are often implemented in, or protected by, hardware.

Industry standards developed by the TCG define the capabilities of a set of fundamental roots of trust, and describe how to use those roots of trust in a variety of architectures and use cases. Many of the use cases supported by TCG technologies and specifications focus on one or more of the following areas: 1) device identity, 2) cryptographic key or credential storage, and 3) attestation of the system state.

Technologies supporting TCG-developed standards are deployed enterprise-class clients and servers, storage devices, embedded systems, and virtualized devices. Families of relevant TCG standards and specifications include:

- Trusted Platform Module (TPM): A TPM is a cryptographic module that can, among other capabilities, establish device identity in a platform, provide secure storage for keys and credentials, and support the measurement and reporting of the system state. The TPM 2.0 Library Specification provides the general architecture and command set for TPMs, with platform-specific specifications detailing how a TPM can be implemented in particular classes of systems. ISO/IEC JTC 1 has approved the TPM Library Specification as ISO/IEC 11889:2015 Parts 1-4.

- Trusted Network Connect (TNC): The TCG's TNC Working Group defines specifications that allow network administrators to enforce policies regarding endpoint integrity on devices connected to a network. These specifications were the basis for much of the work in the IETF's Network Endpoint Assessment (NEA) working group, and are highly complimentary to the on-going work in the IETF Security Automation and Continuous Monitoring (SACM) working group.

- Storage: The TCG's Storage Work Group defines specifications that enable standards-based mechanisms to protect data on storage devices, and manage these devices and capabilities. The TCG's storage specifications break out from a common core specification into two Security Subsystem Classes (SSCs): the Opal SSC, which is intended for client devices (e.g., tablets, notebooks and desktops), and the Enterprise SSC, which is intended for high-performance storage systems (e.g., servers).

SECTION 3: CRYPTOGRAPHIC ALGORITHMS

This document describes three types of cryptographic algorithms: cryptographic hash functions, symmetric-key algorithms and asymmetric-key algorithms, which are discussed in Sections 3.1, 3.2 and 3.3, respectively. Other topics to be introduced in this section include the concept of algorithm security strength and algorithm lifetime (see Sections 3.4 and 3.5, respectively).

3.1   Cryptographic Hash Functions

A hash function (also called a hash algorithm) is a cryptographic primitive algorithm that produces a condensed representation of its input (e.g., a message). A hash function takes an input of arbitrary length and outputs a value with a predetermined length. Common names for the output of a hash function include *hash value* and *message digest*.

A cryptographic hash function is a one-way function that is extremely difficult to invert. That is, it is not practical to reverse the process from the hash value back to the input.

Figure 1 depicts the process of generating and verifying a hash value.

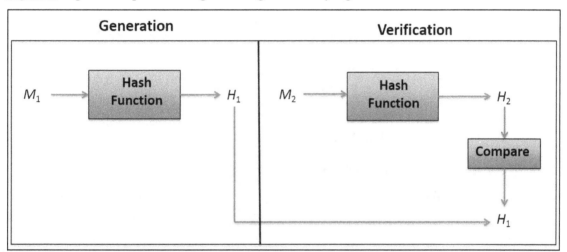

Figure 1: Hash Function Generation and Verification

A hash function is used as follows:

- Hash Generation:

   1. Hash value (H_1) is generated on data (M_1) using the hash function.

   2. M_1 and H_1 are then saved or transmitted.

- Hash Verification:

   1. Hash value (H_2) is generated on the received or retrieved data (M_2) using the same hash function that generated H_1.

   2. H_1 and H_2 are compared. If $H_1 = H_2$, then it can be assumed that M_1 has not changed during storage or transmission.

The above description is for the simplest use of a hash function. Hash functions are usually used in higher-level algorithms, including:

- Keyed-hash message authentication code algorithms (Sections 3.2.2 and 4.2.2.2),

- Digital signature algorithms (Section 4.2.3),

- Key derivation functions (e.g., for key establishment) (Section 5.3.2), and

- Random bit generators (Section 4.4).

Approved hash functions for Federal Government use are specified in FIPS 180[23] and FIPS 202[24].

- FIPS 180 specifies the SHA-1, SHA-224, SHA-256, SHA-384, SHA-512, SHA-512/224 and SHA-512/256 hash functions. Additional guidance for the use of these hash functions is provided in SP 800-106[25] and SP 800-107[26].

  Note that attacks on SHA-1 have indicated that SHA-1 provides less security than originally thought when generating digital signatures (see Section 4.2.3); consequently, SHA-1 is now disallowed for that purpose. However, SHA-1 may continue to be used for most other hash-function applications, including the verification of digital signatures previously signed using SHA-1 as the hash function (see SP 800-131A[27]).

- FIPS 202 specifies SHA3-224, SHA3-256, SHA3-384 and SHA3-512. This FIPS also specifies two extendable-output functions (SHAKE128 and SHAKE256), which are not, in themselves, considered to be hash functions; guidance on their use will be provided in the future.

3.2   Symmetric-Key Algorithms

Symmetric-key algorithms (sometimes called secret-key algorithms) use a single key to both apply cryptographic protection and to remove or check the protection. For example, the key used to encrypt data (i.e., apply protection) is also used to decrypt the encrypted data (i.e., remove the protection); in the case of encryption, the original data is called the plaintext, while the encrypted form of the data is called the ciphertext. The key must be kept secret if the data is to remain protected.

Several classes of symmetric-key algorithms have been approved: those based on block cipher algorithms (e.g., AES) and those based on the use of hash functions (e.g., a keyed-hash message authentication code based on SHA-1).

---

[23] FIPS 180, *Secure Hash Standard (SHS)*.

[24] FIPS 202, *SHA-3 Standard: Permutation-Based Hash and Extendable Output Functions*.

[25] SP 800-106, *Randomized Hashing for Digital Signatures*.

[26] SP 800-107, *Recommendations for Applications Using Approved Hash Algorithms*.

[27] SP 800-131A, *Transitions: Recommendation for Transitioning the Use of Cryptographic Algorithms and Key Lengths*.

Symmetric-key algorithms are used for:

- Encryption to provide data confidentiality (see Section 4.1),

- Authentication to provide assurance of data integrity and the source of the data (see Section 4.2),

- Key derivation (see Section 5.3.2),

- Key wrapping (see Section 5.3.5), and

- Random bit generation (see Section 4.4).

When using a symmetric-key algorithm, a unique key needs to be generated for each cryptographic relationship[28] and for each purpose (e.g., encryption, data integrity authentication and key wrapping). Technically, the same key can be used for multiple purposes when the same algorithm is used, but this is usually ill-advised, as the use of the same key for two different cryptographic processes (e.g., HMAC and key derivation using the same hash function) may weaken the security provided by one or both of the processes. However, exceptions to this rule have been approved (see Section 4.3).

As an example of the number of keys required for the use of symmetric-key algorithms, suppose that there are four entities (A, B, C, and D) that need to communicate using encryption, with each pair of entities using a different encryption key. There are six possible pair-wise relationships (A-B, A-C, A-D, B-C, B-D, and C-D), so, at least six keys are required[29]. If, instead, there are 1000 entities that wish to communicate with each other, there are 499 500 possible pair-wise relationships, and at least one unique key would be required for each relationship. If more than one algorithm, key length or purpose is to be supported (e.g., both encryption and key wrapping), then additional keys will be needed. Each entity must keep all its symmetric keys secret and protect their integrity. The need for a large number of keying relationships is a significant problem; methods for mitigating this problem are discussed in Section 5.

Several symmetric-key algorithms have been **approved** by NIST for the protection of sensitive data. However, some of these algorithms are no longer approved for applying cryptographic protection (e.g., encryption), but may continue to be used for processing already-protected information (e.g., decryption), providing that the risk of doing so is acceptable (e.g., there is reason to believe that a key was not compromised). See SP 800-57, Part 1 and SP 800-131A for more information about the acceptability of using the different cryptographic algorithms.

---

[28] A cryptographic relationship exists when two or more parties can communicate using the same key and algorithm. A relationship may be one-to-one or one-to-many (e.g., broadcast).

[29] Although only six cryptographic relationships are used in the example, different keys may be required by some protocols for each communication direction, i.e., a different key may be required for communications sent from A to B than is used for communications sent from B to A.

3.2.1 Block Cipher Algorithms

A block cipher algorithm is used with a single key in an **approved** mode of operation to both apply cryptographic protection (e.g., encrypt) and to subsequently process the protected information (e.g., decrypt). Several block cipher algorithms have been approved by NIST as cryptographic primitives, some of which may no longer be approved for applying cryptographic protection. However, they may still be needed for processing information that was previously protected (e.g., they may be needed for decrypting previously encrypted information).

The block cipher algorithms are discussed in Sections 3.2.1.1 through 3.2.1.4. The **approved** modes of operation are discussed in Section 3.2.1.5.

3.2.1.1 Data Encryption Standard (DES)

The Data Encryption Standard (DES) became effective in July 1977, and was the first NIST-**approved** cryptographic algorithm. It was reaffirmed several times, but due to advances in computer power and speeds, the strength of the DES algorithm is no longer sufficient to adequately protect Federal Government information. Therefore, DES was withdrawn as an **approved** algorithm in 2005 (i.e., the use of DES is no longer approved for encryption or otherwise applying cryptographic protection). However, the DES "cryptographic engine" continues to be used as a component function of TDEA (see the next section).

3.2.1.2 Triple Data Encryption Algorithm (TDEA)

The Triple Data Encryption Algorithm (TDEA), also known as Triple DES, uses the DES cryptographic engine to transform data in three operations. TDEA is specified in SP 800-67.

TDEA encrypts data in blocks of 64 bits, using three keys that define a key bundle. The use of TDEA using three distinctly different (i.e., mathematically independent) keys is **approved** and is commonly known as three-key TDEA (also referred to as 3TDEA or 3TDES).

Other variations of TDEA, where two or three of the keys are identical, are no longer approved for applying cryptographic protection because of increased computing power or weaknesses in the algorithm.

3.2.1.3 SKIPJACK

SKIPJACK is referenced in FIPS 185[30] and specified in a classified document. SKIPJACK is no longer considered adequate for the protection of federal information and has been withdrawn as a FIPS. The use of SKIPJACK for applying cryptographic protection (e.g., encryption) is **not approved**, although it is permissible to use the algorithm for decrypting information.

---

[30] FIPS 185, *Escrowed Encryption Standard.*

3.2.1.4   Advanced Encryption Standard (AES)

The Advanced Encryption Standard (AES) was developed as a replacement for DES and is the preferred block cipher algorithm for new products. AES is specified in FIPS 197. AES operates on 128-bit blocks of data, using 128-, 192- or 256-bit keys.

Note that the performance of AES is significantly better than that of TDEA.

3.2.1.5   Modes of Operation

With a symmetric-key block cipher algorithm, the same input block will always produce the same output block when the same key is used. Furthermore, certain kinds of data patterns in the plaintext, such as repeated blocks, would be apparent in the ciphertext. To counteract these properties, modes of operation have been specified to use a block cipher algorithm to provide an information service, such as confidentiality or integrity protection.

These modes combine the cryptographic primitive algorithm with a symmetric key and variable starting values (commonly known as initialization vectors) to perform a cryptographic service (e.g., the encryption of a message). **Approved** modes for block cipher algorithms have been specified in the SP 800-38 series of publications and include modes for:

- Encryption, as specified in SP 800-38A, SP 800-38E and SP 800-38G (see Section 4.1),

- Authentication, as specified in SP 800-38B (see Section 4.2.2.1),

- Authenticated encryption, as specified in SP 800-38C and SP 800-38D (see Section 4.3), and

- Key wrapping, as specified in SP 800-38F (see Section 5.3.5).

3.2.2   Hash-based Symmetric-key Algorithms

A symmetric-key algorithm based on the use of a hash function has been specified in FIPS 198[31]. This algorithm, known as HMAC, has been **approved** for use with any **approved** hash function specified in FIPS 180 or FIPS 202. Guidance on the use of the hash functions specified in FIPS 180 for HMAC is provided in SP 800-107.

3.3   Asymmetric-Key Algorithms

Asymmetric-key algorithms (often called public-key algorithms) use a pair of keys (i.e., a key pair): a public key and a private key that are mathematically related to each other. The public key may be made public without reducing the security of the process, but the private key must remain secret if the data is to retain its cryptographic protection. Even though there is a relationship between the two keys, the private key cannot efficiently be determined based on knowledge of the public key.

---

[31] FIPS 198, *Keyed Hash Message Authentication Code (HMAC)*.

One of the keys of the key pair is used to apply cryptographic protection, and the other key is used to remove or verify that protection. The key to use depends on the algorithm used and the service to be provided. For example, a digital signature is computed using a private key, and the signature is verified using the public key (i.e., the protection is applied using the private key and verified using the corresponding public key). For those asymmetric algorithms also capable of encryption[32], the encryption is performed using the public key, and the decryption is performed using the private key (i.e., the protection is applied using the public key and removed using the private key).

Asymmetric-key algorithms are used primarily for data integrity authentication and source authentication (see Section 4.2), and for key establishment (see Section 5.3). These algorithms tend to be much slower than symmetric-key algorithms, so are not used to process large amounts of data. However, when used for key establishment (see Section 5), there are methods that combine the use of symmetric and asymmetric algorithms to reduce the number of keys required for establishing cryptographic relationships.

Key pairs for asymmetric-key algorithms should be generated for each purpose (e.g., one key pair for generating and verifying digital signatures, and a different key pair for key establishment). Technically, it is sometimes possible to use the same key pair for more than one purpose, but this is ill-advised, as the use of the same key pair for two different cryptographic purposes (e.g., digital signatures and key establishment) may weaken the security provided by one or both of the processes.

The use of asymmetric-key algorithms requires the establishment of fewer initial keys than the use of symmetric-key algorithms. As an example, suppose that an entity wants to generate digital signatures and participate in a key-establishment process using its own key pair[33]; a key pair needs to be generated for each purpose. If there are six entities that intend to both generate digital signatures and participate in the key-establishment process, then six key pairs are needed for digital signature generation, and another six key pairs are needed for key establishment, for a total of twelve key pairs. For 1000 entities, 1000 key pairs of each would be needed for each purpose, for a total of 2000 key pairs. A unique key pair does not need to be generated for each relationship; recall that for symmetric-key algorithms, a unique key needs to be generated for each relationship (see Section 3.2). If multiple public-key algorithms or key lengths are to be used for either process, then additional key pairs will be required.

The private key is retained by the entity who "owns" the key pair; it must be kept secret and its integrity protected. The public key is usually distributed to other entities and requires integrity protection; this is often accomplished by using a public-key certificate, as discussed in Section 5.2.3. When a public-key certificate is used, the certificate provides the integrity protection for the public key, so the burden of key protection by each entity is limited to only those private keys owned by the entity.

---

[32] Not all public-key algorithms are capable of multiple functions, e.g., both encryption and decryption, and the generation and verification of digital signatures.

[33] Note that some key-establishment schemes do not require that all parties have key pairs, so some parties will not need a key pair for key establishment.

Some asymmetric-key algorithms use domain parameters, which are additional values necessary for the use of the cryptographic algorithm. These values are mathematically related to each other and to the keys with which they will be used. Domain parameters are usually public and are used by a community of users for a substantial period of time. These domain parameters are either contained within or referenced by a certificate containing a public key.

The secure use of asymmetric-key algorithms is dependent on users obtaining certain assurances:

- Assurance of domain-parameter validity (for those algorithms requiring domain parameters) provides confidence that the domain parameters are mathematically correct,
- Assurance of public-key validity provides confidence that the public key appears to be a suitable key, and
- Assurance of private-key possession provides confidence that the party that is supposedly the owner of the private key really has the key.

3.3.1 DSA

The Digital Signature Algorithm (DSA) is **approved** and specified in FIPS 186. This algorithm is used to generate and verify digital signatures using finite-fields. FIPS 186 defines methods for generating DSA domain parameters and key pairs, and specifies the key lengths to be used for secure interoperability and the algorithms to be used for digital-signature generation and verification.

3.3.2 ECDSA

The Elliptic Curve Digital Signature Algorithm (ECDSA) is **approved** within FIPS 186, but actually specified within American National Standard (ANS) X9.62[34]. The basic signature and verification algorithms are the same as those used for DSA, except that the mathematics is based on the use of elliptic curves, rather than finite fields. FIPS 186 provides guidance for the use of ECDSA within the Federal Government, as well as providing recommended elliptic curves to facilitate interoperability and security. An advantage of using ECDSA is that the key lengths are considerably shorter than those used for DSA and RSA, requiring less storage space and transmission bandwidth, and the execution of the algorithm is generally faster than DSA and RSA

ANS X9.62 includes specifications for the generation of the ECDSA domain parameters and key pairs, as well as the algorithms for digital signature generation and verification. FIPS 186 defines the key lengths to be used for secure interoperability, provides additional guidance on the use of random bit generators to generate the key pairs, and recommends elliptic curves for use by the Federal Government. Note that the same elliptic curves are also included in ANS X9.62.

---

[34] ANS X9.62, *Public Key Cryptography for the Financial Services Industry: The Elliptic Curve Digital Signature Algorithm (ECDSA).*

3.3.3 RSA

The RSA algorithm is **approved** for the generation and verification of digital signatures in FIPS 186] and specified in PKCS 1[35] and ANS X9.31[36]. FIPS 186 includes restrictions on the use of RSA to generate digital signatures, methods to generate RSA key pairs, and defines the key lengths to be used for secure interoperability.

The RSA primitive can be used for key establishment, as well as for the generation and verification of digital signatures. Its use for key establishment is specified in SP 800-56B[37]; that publication specifies **approved** methods for both key agreement and key transport (see Section 5.3 for further information on key establishment, key agreement and key transport).

The key pairs used for RSA digital-signature generation and verification, and for RSA key establishment are generated in the same way, but need to be different for each purpose.

3.3.4 Diffie-Hellman and MQV

Diffie-Hellman (DH) and MQV[38] are two classes of key-establishment algorithms used for key agreement (see Section 5.3.3). The use of these algorithms for key agreement is specified in SP 800-56A[39] using both finite-fields and elliptic-curves. For elliptic-curve key pairs and domain parameters, the methods for generating those key pairs and domain parameters are specified in ANS X9.62 using the same methods used to generate ECDSA key pairs and domain parameters.

The recommended elliptic curves for elliptic-curve DH and MQV are the same as those provided in FIPS 186 for ECDSA.

3.4 Algorithm Security Strength

The security strength of a cryptographic algorithm is measured by an attacker's difficulty in breaking the algorithm. Breaking a cryptographic algorithm can be defined as defeating some aspect of the protection that the algorithm is intended to provide. For example, a block cipher encryption algorithm that is used to protect the confidentiality of data is broken if, with an acceptable amount of work, it is possible to determine the value of its key or to recover the plaintext from the ciphertext without knowledge of the key.

---

[35] Public Key Cryptography Standard #1.

[36] ANS X9.31, *Digital Signatures Using Reversible Public Key Cryptography For The Financial Services Industry (RDSA)*. This standard has been withdrawn as an ANSI standard.

[37] SP 800-56B, *Recommendation for Pair-wise Key Establishment Schemes Using Integer Factorization Cryptography*.

[38] Menezes–Qu–Vanstone.

[39] SP 800-56A, *Recommendation for Pair-Wise Key-Establishment Schemes Using Discrete Logarithm Cryptography*.

SP 800-57, Part 1 provides the current estimates for the security strengths that can be provided by the **approved** cryptographic algorithms; these strengths have been determined with respect to specific key lengths.

The **approved** security strengths for federal applications are 112, 128, 192 and 256 bits. Note that a security strength of 80 bits was previously approved as well. Since it is no longer considered as providing adequate protection, the use of algorithms and keys providing a security strength of 80 bits is **no longer approved** for applying cryptographic protection (e.g., encrypting data). However, algorithms and keys providing 80 bits of strength can be used for processing data that was previously protected at that strength (e.g., for decryption).

Appropriate algorithms, key lengths, and key generation and handling methods need to be used to actually support those security strengths, and are further discussed in Section 5.1.4.

3.5 Algorithm Lifetime

Over time, algorithms may be successfully attacked so that the algorithm no longer provides the desired protection. The attack could be on the algorithm itself, or could be on the algorithm with a specific key length. In the latter case, the use of a longer key may prevent a successful attack, or at least delay it for a period of time.

When selecting the algorithms and key lengths to be used for an application, the length of time for which the data needs to be protected should be taken into account so that a suitable algorithm and key length is used. SP 800-57, Part 1 provides a current estimate of the time frames during which the **approved** algorithms and key lengths are considered to be secure. The algorithms and key lengths used for cryptographic protection need to fall within the estimated time frame. However, these estimates are just that – estimates. It is possible that an advance in technology (e.g., the use of quantum computers and algorithms) or cryptanalysis could occur prior to the end date of that time frame. It is often the case that these advances are initially impractical or limited in their threat. It is recommended that an organization have a transition strategy for addressing this problem if it occurs, including assessing the risk for the compromise of the organization's data, and transitioning to a new algorithm or key length, as appropriate.

SECTION 4: CRYPTOGRAPHIC SERVICES

All sensitive information requires integrity protection, and confidentiality protection may be required as well. This section discusses the cryptographic services that can be provided for the protection of sensitive data other than keys. These services include data confidentiality, data integrity authentication and source authentication, including non-repudiation. The protection and management of the keys used while providing these cryptographic services are discussed in Section 5.

Ideally, cryptographic services would be provided using as few algorithms as possible. For example, AES could be used to provide confidentiality (Section 4.1), data integrity authentication (Section 4.2), key wrapping (Section 5.3.5) and as the basis for a random bit generator (see Section 4.4). However, this may not be as practical as it first appears, as other algorithms may also be available that are needed for different applications and that provide other security properties.

4.1 Data Confidentiality

Encryption is used to provide confidentiality for data. The unprotected form of the data is called plaintext. Encryption transforms the data into ciphertext, and ciphertext can be transformed back into plaintext using decryption. Data encryption and decryption are generally provided using symmetric-key block cipher algorithms. The **approved** symmetric-key algorithms for data encryption are: AES and TDEA (see Section 3.2.1.4 and Section 3.2.1.2, respectively). Decryption of the ciphertext is performed using the algorithm and key that were used to encrypt the plaintext. Unauthorized recipients of the ciphertext who know the cryptographic algorithm but do not have the correct key should not be able to decrypt the ciphertext. However, anyone who has the key and the cryptographic algorithm can easily decrypt the ciphertext and obtain the original plaintext.

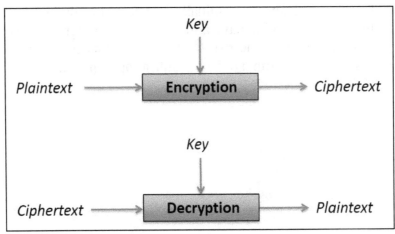

Figure 2: Encryption and Decryption

Figure 2 depicts the encryption and decryption processes. The plaintext and a key are used by the encryption process to produce the ciphertext. To decrypt, the ciphertext and the same key are used by the decryption process to recover the plaintext data.

Note that asymmetric-key algorithms could also be used to encrypt and decrypt data, but because these algorithms are slow in comparison to block cipher algorithms, they are not normally used to encrypt and decrypt general data; they can, however, be used to protect keys, as discussed in Section 5.

As discussed in Section 3.2.1.5, encryption is performed using a block cipher algorithm and a mode of operation. The **approved** modes of operation for encryption are specified in:

- SP 800-38A for AES and TDEA: the Electronic Codebook (ECB), Cipher Block Chaining (CBC), Cipher Feedback (CFB), Counter (CTR), and Output Feedback (OFB) modes,

- SP 800-38E for AES: the XTS-AES mode (for protecting the confidentiality of data on storage devices only), and

- SP 800-38G for AES: the FF1 and FF3 modes for Format Preserving Encryption.

Additional modes that provide both confidentiality and authentication (as discussed in Section 4.2) are discussed in Section 4.3.

4.2   Data Integrity and Source Authentication

Data integrity (often referred to as simply *integrity*) is concerned with whether or not data has changed between two specified times (e.g., between the time when the data was created, stored and/or transmitted, and the time when it was retrieved and/or received). While data integrity cannot be guaranteed, the use of data integrity codes provides a means to detect changes with a high probability. A data integrity code is computed on data when it is created, before storage or before transmission, and computed again when the data is retrieved or received. Verification that these computations agree provides a measure of assurance of data integrity. In cryptographic literature, this process is called *message* (or data) *authentication.*

Source authentication is a process used to provide assurance of the source of information. Source authentication includes identity authentication, which provides assurance to one of the parties in a communication (say, Bob) that he is receiving data from or providing data to another specific party (say, Alice). Depending on the method used, source authentication could also support non-repudiation, whereby both Bob and some third party (say, Carl) have some assurance that the data came from Alice.

Cryptography can be used to provide these services, but the same algorithm may not provide all of them. Hash functions, as discussed in Section 4.2.1, can be used to provide some assurance of data integrity. Message Authentication Code (MAC) algorithms, as discussed in Section 4.2.2, can provide both data integrity and source authentication services. Digital signature algorithms can be used to provide data integrity and source authentication services, as well as supporting non-repudiation, but at a higher performance cost (see Section 4.2.3).

4.2.1 Hash Functions

A hash function is used to generate a hash value that can provide some assurance of the integrity of the data over which the hash value is generated. However, if a hash function is used alone (e.g., without the use of a secret key, as is the case of HMAC, or in conjunction with the generation of digital signatures), there is no assurance that the data has not been altered by an adversary and a new hash value computed. Therefore, the use of a hash function alone for providing integrity protection is not recommended unless there is a very low risk of this scenario (e.g., when data is provided by a trusted source, and the hash value is used only to determine changes that may occur because of a degraded transmission medium).

4.2.2 Message Authentication Code Algorithms

A Message Authentication Code algorithm and a cryptographic key are used to generate a message authentication code (MAC) that can be used to provide assurance of data integrity and source authentication. A MAC is a cryptographic checksum on the data that can provide assurance that the data has not changed or been altered since some point in time, and that the MAC was computed by the party or parties sharing the key. Typically, MACs are used between two or more parties that share the same secret key to authenticate information exchanged between those parties; the use of MACs to provide data integrity and source authentication depends on limiting knowledge of the secret key to only those parties. Since a MAC key is shared among a community of users (e.g., two or more parties), only those parties sharing the key can compute a correct MAC on given data.

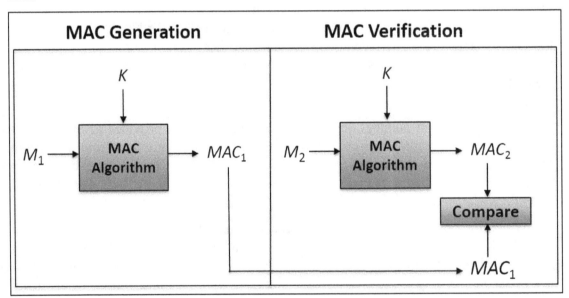

Figure 3: Message Authentication and Verification

Figure 3 depicts the use of MACs:

- A MAC (MAC_1) is computed on data (M_1) using a key (K). M_1 and MAC_1 are then saved or transmitted.

- At a later time, the integrity of the retrieved or received data is checked by labeling the retrieved or received data as M_2 and computing a MAC (MAC_2) on M_2 using the same key (K).

- If MAC_1 is the same as MAC_2, then it can be assumed that M_2 is the same as the original data (M_1) (i.e., $M_1 = M_2$). The verifying party also knows that only a party that shares the key could have correctly generated the MAC.

For example, if two parties (e.g., A and B) share a key, party A generates the MAC and sends it to party B, and party B successfully verifies the received MAC, then party B knows that party A generated the original MAC, and source authentication has been accomplished. However, if three parties share the key (e.g., A, B and C), party A generates the MAC to be sent to party B, and party B successfully verifies the received MAC; party B knows that either party A or party C generated the original MAC, but has no proof of which one. Note that this may be acceptable for some applications.

MACs are used to detect data modifications that occur between the initial generation of the MAC and the verification of the received MAC. They do not detect errors that occur before the MAC is originally generated.

Assurance of data integrity is frequently provided using non-cryptographic techniques known as error detection codes. However, these codes can be altered by an adversary to the adversary's benefit. The use of an **approved** cryptographic mechanism, such as a MAC, addresses this problem. That is, the assurance of integrity provided by a MAC is based on the assumption that it is not likely that anyone could correctly generate a MAC without knowing the cryptographic key. An adversary without knowledge of the key will be unable to modify data and then generate a verifiable MAC on the modified data. It is therefore crucial that MAC keys be kept secret.

Two types of algorithms for computing a MAC have been **approved** for Federal Government use: MAC algorithms that are based on symmetric-key block cipher algorithms, and MAC algorithms that are based on hash functions.

4.2.2.1 MACs Based on Block Cipher Algorithms

The SP 800-38 series of publications includes modes for the generation of MACs:

- SP 800-38B[40] defines the CMAC mode for computing a MAC using the NIST-**approved** block-cipher algorithms: AES and TDEA.

- SP 800-38D[41] defines the GMAC mode for the computation of a MAC using AES.

- Modes providing both confidentiality (i.e., encryption) and authentication (i.e., computing a MAC) in a single operation are also defined (see Section 4.3).

---

[40] SP 800-38B, *Recommendation for Block Cipher Modes of Operation: The CMAC Mode for Authentication.*

[41] SP 800-38D, *Recommendation for Block Cipher Modes of Operation: Galois/Counter Mode (GCM) and GMAC.*

4.2.2.2 MACs Based on Hash Functions

FIPS 198[42] defines a MAC (HMAC) that uses a cryptographic hash function in combination with a secret key. HMAC must be used with an **approved** cryptographic hash function (see Section 4.2.1). The security associated with the use of HMAC is discussed in SP 800-107[43].

4.2.3 Digital Signature Algorithms

A digital signature algorithm is used with a pair of keys – a private key and a public key – to generate and verify digital signatures. The private key is used to generate signatures and must be known only by the signer (the key-pair owner); the public key is used to verify the signatures. Because of the design of the algorithm, and the methods for generating key pairs, the public key cannot efficiently be used to determine the private key. Because two keys are required for the generation and verification process, digital signature algorithms are classified as asymmetric-key algorithms.

A digital signature is represented in a computer as a string of bits and is an electronic analogue of a hand-written signature that can be verified by anyone with access to the public key. The signature can be used to provide assurance of data integrity and source authentication, and to support non-repudiation.

Each signer possesses a private and public key pair. Signature generation (with a verifiable digital signature) can be performed only by the party that has access to the private key. Anyone that knows the public key can verify the signature by employing the associated public key. The security of a digital-signature system is dependent on maintaining the secrecy of the signer's private key. Therefore, signers must guard against the unauthorized acquisition of their private keys.

Digital signatures offer protection that is not available by using alternative signature techniques. One such alternative is a digitized signature. A digitized signature is generated by converting a visual form of a handwritten signature to an electronic image (e.g., by scanning it into a computer). Although a digitized signature resembles its handwritten counterpart when printed, it does not provide the same protection as a digital signature. Digitized signatures can be forged and can be duplicated and appended to other electronic data; digitized signatures cannot be used to determine if information has been altered after it is signed. Digital signatures, however, are computed on each message using a private key known only by the signer. Each different message signed by the signer will have a different digital signature. Even small changes to the message will result in a different signature. If an adversary does not know the private key, the adversary cannot generate a valid signature (i.e., a signature that can be verified using the public key that corresponds to the private key used to generate the signature).

Figure 4 depicts the generation and verification of digital signatures. A digital signature algorithm includes a signature generation process and a signature verification process:

---

[42] FIPS 198-1, *The Keyed-Hash Message Authentication Code (HMAC)*.

[43] SP 800-107, *Recommendation for Applications Using Approved Hash Algorithms*.

- Signature generation:
  - A hash function (see Section 3.1) is used in the signature generation process to obtain a hash value, which is a condensed version of the data to be signed (i.e., shown as M_1 for signature generation in Figure 4).

  - The hash value is then input to the signature generation process, along with a private key, to generate the digital signature (shown as DS_1 in Figure 4).

  - The digital signature (DS_1) is provided to the verifier, along with the signed data (M_1).

- Signature verification: The receiver of the data and signature verifies the signature as follows:

  - The received data (M_2) is hashed using the same hash function to produce another hash value.

  - The newly computed hash value and the received signature (DS_2) are input to the signature verification process, along with the the signer's public key. The output of this process is an indication of whether or not the signature is valid or invalid for the received message (M_2).

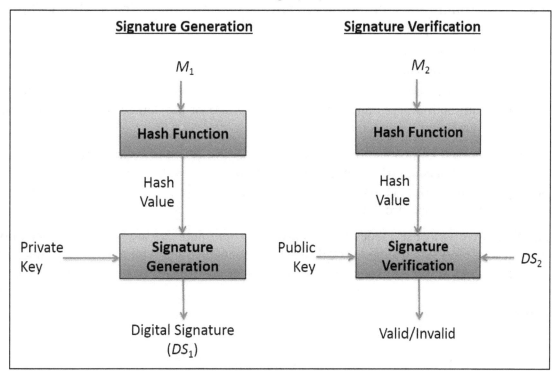

Figure 4: Digital Signature Generation and Verification

Note that the details of the signature generation and verification processes are different for each approved algorithm. Also, note that M_2 is used in the verification process rather than M_1, and DS_2 is used rather than DS_1 because of the possibility that M_1 and DS_1 could have been deliberately or accidentally modified before the verification process performed by the receiver.

FIPS 186 specifies methods for generating and verifying digital signatures using asymmetric (public-key) cryptography. The FIPS includes three digital signature algorithms:

- The Digital Signature Algorithm (DSA) (see Section 3.3.1),

- The Elliptic Curve Digital Signature Algorithm (ECDSA) (see Section 3.3.2), and

- RSA (see Section 3.3.3).

The digital signature algorithms are used in conjunction with the hash functions specified in FIPS 180[44] and FIPS 202. Each of these algorithms requires obtaining assurances about the domain parameters and/or keys used, as discussed in Section 3.3; SP 800-89[45] provides methods for obtaining these required assurances when using digital signatures.

In many cases, determining when a digital signature was generated is important. For example, it may be important to determine whether a document was signed before a certain date, e.g., which of two wills was signed closest to and prior to the date that a person died. SP 800-102[46] provides guidance on establishing when a digital signature was generated.

4.3   Combining Confidentiality and Authentication in a Block-Cipher Mode of Operation

Confidentiality and authentication can be provided using either two separate block-cipher algorithms (e.g., AES in the CBC mode for encryption and HMAC for authentication) or in a single block-cipher mode of operation. Note that in this discussion, authentication is used to obtain both an assurance of data integrity and of the source of the data that has been cryptographically protected.

If encryption and authentication are performed as two separate operations (see Sections 4.1 and 4.2, respectively), two distinct keys are required. If care is not taken in performing these operations (e.g., performing the operations in the right order), vulnerabilities can be introduced that may allow attacks.

An alternative is to use modes that both encrypt and authenticate in a single operation using a single key; such a mode is called an "authenticated-encryption" mode. Using such modes requires fewer keys and is generally faster than using two separate operations. Two authenticated-encryption modes have been defined for AES (no such mode has been defined for TDEA):

- SP 800-38C[47] specifies the CCM mode, and

- SP 800-38D[48] defines the Galois/Counter mode (GCM).

---

[44] FIPS 180, *Secure Hash Standard (SHS)*.

[45] SP 800-89, *Recommendation for Obtaining Assurances for Digital Signature Applications*.

[46] SP 800-102, *Recommendation for Digital Signature Timeliness*.

[47] SP 800-38C, *Recommendation for Block Cipher Modes of Operation: the CCM Mode for Authentication and Confidentiality*.

4.4   Random Bit Generation

Cryptography and security applications make extensive use of random numbers and random bits. For cryptography, random values are needed to generate cryptographic keys. The term "entropy" is used to describe the amount of randomness in a value, and the amount of entropy determines how hard it is to guess that value.

There are two classes of random bit generators (RBGs): Non-Deterministic Random Bit Generators (NRBGs), sometimes called true random number (or bit) generators, and Deterministic Random Bit Generators (DRBGs), sometimes called pseudorandom bit (or number) generators. Each RBG is dependent on the use of an entropy source to provide unpredictable bits that are outside of human control; these bits are acquired from some physical source, such as thermal noise, ring oscillators or hard-drive seek times. An NRBG is dependent on the availability of new, unused entropy bits produced by the entropy source for every NRBG output. A DRBG is initially "seeded" with entropy produced by an entropy source or using an **approved** method that depends on an entropy source (e.g., an NRBG); depending on the application, the DRBG may or may not receive additional entropy during operation (e.g., by being reseeded).

Several publications have been developed or are currently under development for random-bit generation:

- SP 800-90A[49] specifies **approved** DRBG algorithms, based on the use of hash functions and block-cipher algorithms; DRBGs must be initialized from a randomness source (e.g., an entropy source or an NRBG) that provides sufficient entropy for the security strength(s) to be supported by the DRBG.

- SP 800-90B[50], which is currently under development, discusses entropy sources, including the health tests needed to determine that the entropy source has not failed and tests to estimate how much entropy that the entropy source can reliably provide.

- SP 800-90C[51] provides constructions for the design and implementation of NRBGs and DRBGs from the algorithms in SP 800-90A and the entropy sources designed in accordance with SP 800-90B. Note that the NRBGs are constructed to include a DRBG algorithm from SP 800-90A to provide a fallback capability if an entropy source failure is not immediately detected.

- SP 800-22[52] discusses some aspects of selecting and testing random and pseudorandom number generators. This document includes some criteria for

---

[48] SP 800-38D, *Recommendation for Block Cipher Modes of Operation: Galois/Counter Mode (GCM) and GMAC*.

[49] SP 800-90A, *Random Number Generation Using Deterministic Random Bit Generator Mechanisms*.

[50] SP 800-90B, *Recommendation for the Entropy Sources Used for Random Bit Generation*.

[51] SP 800-90C, *Recommendation for Random Bit Generator (RBG) Constructions*.

[52] SP 800-22, *A Statistical Test Suite for Random and Pseudorandom Number Generators for Cryptographic Applications*.

characterizing and selecting appropriate generators, discusses statistical testing and its relation to cryptanalysis and provides some recommended statistical tests. These tests may be useful as a first step in determining whether or not a generator is suitable for a particular cryptographic application. However, for federal applications, the RBGs must be validated for compliance to FIPS 140 and the appropriate parts of SP 800-90.

4.5   Symmetric vs. Asymmetric Cryptography

As discussed in Sections 3.2 and 3.3, when large numbers of cryptographic relationships are required, the number of initial symmetric keys that will be required may be significantly larger than the number of public/private key pairs required.

However, the primary advantage of symmetric-key cryptography is speed. Symmetric-key algorithms are generally significantly faster than asymmetric-key algorithms, and the keys are shorter in length for the same security strength; the key length may be an important consideration if memory for storing the keys, or the bandwidth for transporting the keys is limited. In addition, advances in cryptanalysis and computational efficiency have tended to reduce the level of protection provided by public-key cryptography more rapidly than that provided by symmetric-key cryptography. Also, in a potential post-quantum world, the currently approved asymmetric-key algorithms will not provide adequate protection.

Since asymmetric-key (i.e., public-key) cryptography requires fewer keys overall, and symmetric-key cryptography is significantly faster, a hybrid approach is often used, whereby asymmetric-key algorithms are used for the generation and verification of digital signatures and for key establishment, while symmetric-key algorithms are used for all other purposes (e.g., encryption), especially those involving the protection of large amounts of data. For example, an asymmetric-key system can be used to establish a symmetric key via a key-agreement or key-transport process (see Sections 5.3.3 and 5.3.4, respectively), after which the symmetric key is used to encrypt files or messages.

In some situations, asymmetric-key cryptography is not necessary, and symmetric-key cryptography alone is sufficient. This includes environments where secure symmetric-key establishment can take place using symmetric keys already shared between entities, environments where a single authority knows and manages all the keys, and in single-user environments.

In general, asymmetric cryptography is best suited for an open, multi-user environment.

SECTION 5: KEY MANAGEMENT

The proper management of cryptographic keys is essential to the effective use of cryptography for security. Keys are analogous to the combination of a safe. If a safe combination becomes known by an adversary, that safe provides no security against penetration by that adversary. Similarly, poor key management may easily compromise strong algorithms. Ultimately, the security of information protected by cryptography directly depends on the strength of the keys, the effectiveness of mechanisms and protocols associated with keys, and the protection afforded to the keys themselves. All keys need to be protected against modification (i.e., their integrity needs to be preserved), and secret and private keys (i.e., keys used by symmetric and asymmetric algorithms, respectively) need to be protected against unauthorized disclosure (i.e., their confidentiality needs to be maintained).

Key management provides the foundation for the secure generation, storage, distribution/establishment, use and destruction of keys, and is essential at all phases of a key's life. If a strong algorithm is used to encrypt data using keys that are properly generated, then the protection of that data can subsequently be reduced to just protecting the keys, i.e. the security of information protected by cryptography directly depends on the protection afforded the keys. Therefore, a Cryptographic Key Management System (CKMS) is required for managing the keys.

5.1 General Key Management Guidance

Several publications have been developed to provide general key-management guidance: SP 800-57 (see Section 5.1.1), FIPS 140 (see Section 5.1.2), and SP 800-131A (see Section 5.1.3).

5.1.1 Recommendation for Key Management

SP 800-57[53] provides general guidance on the management of cryptographic keys: their generation, use, and eventual destruction. Related topics, such as algorithm selection and appropriate key size, and cryptographic policy are also included in SP 800-57, which consists of three parts:

- SP 800-57, Part 1, *General Guidance*, contains basic key-management guidance, including:

  - The protection required for keying material;

  - Key life-cycle responsibilities;

  - Key backup, archiving and recovery;

  - Changing keys;

  - Cryptoperiods (i.e., the appropriate lengths of time that keys are to be used);

  - Accountability and auditing;

---

[53] SP 800-57, *Recommendation for Key Management*.

- o Contingency planning; and

- o Key compromise recovery (e.g., by generating new keys).

Federal agencies have a variety of information that they have determined to require cryptographic protection; the sensitivity of the information and the periods of time that the protection is required also vary. To this end, NIST has established four security strengths for the protection of information: 112, 128, 192 and 256 bits[54]. These security strengths have been assigned to the **approved** cryptographic algorithms and key sizes, and dates have been projected during which the use of these algorithms and key sizes is anticipated to be secure. For further information, see SP 800-131A.

Agencies need to determine the length of time that cryptographic protection is required before selecting an algorithm and key size with the appropriate security strength.

Note that SP 800-57, Part 1 will be updated if the guidance provided therein is no longer valid (e.g., an algorithm no longer provides adequate security).

- SP 800-57, Part 2, *Best Practices for Key Management Organization*, contains:

  - o A generic key-management infrastructure,

  - o Guidance for the development of organizational key-management policy statements and key-management practices statements,

  - o An identification of key-management information that needs to be incorporated into security plans for general support systems and major applications that employ cryptography, and

  - o An identification of key-management information that needs to be documented for all federal applications of cryptography.

- SP 800-57, Part 3, *Application-Specific Key Management Guidance*, addresses the key management issues associated with currently available cryptographic mechanisms, such as the Public Key infrastructure (PKI), Internet Protocol Security (IPsec), the Transport Layer Security protocol (TLS), Secure/Multipart Internet Mail Extensions (S/MIME), Kerberos, Over-the-Air Rekeying (OTAR), Domain Name System Security Extensions (DNSSEC), Encrypted File Systems and the Secure Shell (SSH) protocol.

Specific guidance is provided regarding:

  - o The recommended and/or allowable algorithm suites and key sizes,

  - o Recommendations for the use of the mechanism in its current form for the protections of federal government information, and

---

[54] A fifth security strength (i.e., 80 bits of security) was acceptable for applying cryptographic protection (e.g., encryption) prior to 2014. However, this strength is not adequate.

o Security considerations that may affect the effectiveness of key-management processes and the cryptographic mechanisms using keys that are generated and managed by those key-management processes.

Note that in the case of TLS, a reference is provided to a separate publication – SP 800-52 [55] – that provides extensive details for using TLS.

New key-management techniques and mechanisms are constantly being developed, and existing key-management mechanisms and techniques are constantly being refined. While the security-guidance information contained in Part 3 will be updated as mechanisms and techniques evolve, new products and technical specifications can always be expected that are not reflected in the current version of the document. Therefore, the context provided may include status information, such as version numbers or implementation status at the time that the document was last revised.

5.1.2 Security Requirements for Cryptographic Modules

FIPS 140 provides minimum security requirements for cryptographic modules that embody or support cryptography in federal information systems. A cryptographic module performs the actual cryptographic computations for a security system protecting sensitive information. The security requirements cover areas related to the secure design and implementation of a cryptographic module, including the module specification; cryptographic module ports and interfaces; roles, services and authentication; finite-state models; physical security; the operational environment; cryptographic key management; electromagnetic interference/electromagnetic compatibility (EMI/EMC); self-tests; design assurance; and the mitigation of attacks.

FIPS 140 is applicable to all federal agencies that use cryptography to protect sensitive information in computer and telecommunications systems. Further information about FIPS 140 and the validation of cryptographic modules is available at http://csrc.nist.gov/groups/STM/cmvp/index.html.

5.1.3 Transitions to New Cryptographic Algorithms and Key Lengths

With the development and publication of SP 800-57, Part 1, NIST provided recommendations for transitioning to new cryptographic algorithms and key lengths because of algorithm breaks or the availability of more powerful computers that could be used to efficiently search for cryptographic keys. SP 800-131A was developed to provide more specific guidance for such transitions. Each algorithm and service is addressed in

---

[55] SP 800-52, *Guidelines for the Selection, Configuration, and Use of Transport Layer Security (TLS) Implementations.*

SP 800-131A, indicating whether its use is acceptable[56], deprecated[57], restricted[58], allowed only for legacy applications[59], or disallowed.

Note that SP 800-131A will be updated if the guidance provided therein is no longer valid (e.g., an algorithm no longer provides adequate security).

5.2   Cryptographic Key Management Systems

Several publications have been developed for the development of key-management systems: SP 800-130[60] (see Section 5.2.1), SP 800-152[61] (see Section 5.2.2) and documents relating to the Public Key Infrastructure used for asymmetric-key cryptography (see Section 5.2.3).

A Cryptographic Key Management System (CKMS) includes policies, procedures, components and devices that are used to protect, manage and distribute cryptographic keys and associated information (called metadata). A CKMS includes all devices or subsystems that can access a key or its metadata. The devices could be computers, cell phones, tablets, or other smart devices, such as cars, alarm systems, or refrigerators.

5.2.1   Key Management Framework

SP 800-130 contains topics that should be considered by a CKMS designer when developing a CKMS design specification. Topics include security policies, cryptographic keys and metadata, interoperability and transitioning, security controls, testing and system assurances, disaster recovery, and security assessments.

For each topic, SP 800-130 specifies one or more documentation requirements that need to be addressed by the designer. SP 800-130 is intended to assist in:

- The definition of the CKMS design by requiring the specification of significant CKMS capabilities,

- Encouraging CKMS designers to consider the factors needed in a comprehensive CKMS,

- Logically comparing different CKMSs and their capabilities,

- Performing security assessments by requiring the specification of implemented and supported CKMS capabilities, and

---

[56] No security risk is known at present.

[57] The use of the algorithm and key length is allowed, but the user must accept some risk.

[58] The use of the algorithm is discouraged, and there are additional restrictions required for use.

[59] The algorithm and key length may be used to process already-protected information, but there may be a risk in doing so.

[60] SP 800-130, *A Framework for Designing Cryptographic Key Management Systems*.

[61] SP 800-152, *A Profile for U. S. Federal Cryptographic Key Management Systems (CKMS)*.

- Forming the basis for the development of Profiles that specify the specific requirements for the CKMS to be used by an organization.

5.2.2 Key Management System Profile

SP 800-152 contains requirements for the design, implementation, procurement, installation, configuration, management, operation and use of a CKMS by and for U.S. federal organizations and their contractors. The Profile is based on SP 800-130 (see Section 5.2.1). SP 800-152 specifies requirements, makes recommendations for federal organizations having special security needs and desiring to augment the base security and key-management services, and suggests additional features that may be desirable to implement and use.

In addition to providing design requirements to be incorporated into a CKMS design, SP 800-152 provides requirements for a Federal CKMS (FCKMS) to be operated by a service provider that may be a federal agency or a third party operating an FCKMS under contract for one or more federal agencies and their contractors.

This Profile is intended to:

- Assist CKMS designers and implementers in supporting appropriate cryptographic algorithms and keys, selecting the metadata associated with the keys, and selecting protocols for protecting sensitive U.S. federal computing applications and data;

- Establish requirements for testing, procurement, installation, configuration, administration, operation, maintenance and usage of the FCKMS;

- Facilitate an easy comparison of one CKMS with another by analyzing their designs and implementations in order to understand how each meets the Framework and Profile requirements; and

- Assist in understanding what is needed to evaluate, procure, install, configure, administer, operate, and use an FCKMS that manages the cryptographic keys that protect sensitive and valuable data obtained, processed, stored, and used by U.S. federal organizations and their contractors.

5.2.3 Public Key Infrastructure

A PKI is a security infrastructure that creates and manages public-key certificates to facilitate the use of public-key (i.e., asymmetric-key) cryptography. To achieve this goal, a PKI needs to perform two basic tasks:

1. Generate and provide public key certificates that bind public keys to the identifier associated with the owner of the corresponding private key[62] and to other required information *after* validating the accuracy of the information to be bound, and

---

[62] The identifier could be the true identity of the owner, or could be an alias or a pseudonym used to represent the owner.

2. Maintain and provide certificate-status information for unexpired and revoked certificates.

Two types of certificates are commonly used: certificates used to provide the public keys that are used to verify digital signatures, and certificates used to provide the public keys used for key management (i.e., key establishment). Each certificate associated with digital signatures provides the public keys of one of the three digital-signature algorithms approved in FIPS 186: DSA, ECDSA or RSA (see Section 3.3). Certificates that convey the public keys to be used for key establishment may be of two types: those that provide a key-agreement public key (see Section 5.3.3), and those that provide a key-transport public key (see Section 5.3.4). Key-usage bits in a certificate indicate the purpose for which the public key is intended to be used.

As discussed in Section 3.3, public keys can be made available to anyone. However, a private key must be maintained under the exclusive control of the owner of that private key[63] (i.e., the user that is authorized to use the private key).

- If a private key that is used to generate digital signatures is lost, the owner can no longer generate digital signatures; some policies may permit users to maintain backup copies of the private key for continuity of operations, but this is not encouraged, so an alternative is to simply generate new key pairs and certificates.

- If the private key used to generate digital signatures is compromised, relying parties can no longer trust the digital signatures generated using that private key (e.g., someone may be using the signature to provide false information).

- If a private key used for key establishment is lost (e.g., a key used for key transport or key agreement), then further key establishment processes cannot be accomplished until the key is recovered or replaced; if the key is needed to recover data protected by the key, then that data is lost unless the key can be recovered. For example, if the key is used to transport a decryption key for encrypted data, and the key is lost, then the encrypted data cannot be decrypted. To ensure that access to critical data is not lost, PKIs often backup the private key-establishment key for possible recovery.

- If a private key used for key establishment is compromised, then any transactions involving that key cannot be trusted (e.g., someone other than the true owner of the private key may be attempting to enter into a supposedly "secure" transaction for some illicit purpose).

5.2.3.1   PKI Components, Relying Parties and Their Responsibilities

For scalability, PKIs are usually implemented with a set of complementary components, each focused on specific aspects of the PKI process. The main PKI tasks are assigned to

---

[63] An exception could be some other trusted entity, such as the owner's organization. In these cases, the organization could be considered to be the *real* owner of the key.

the following logical components; other components are also used to support the PKI, but are not discussed here (see SP 800-32[64] for further discussion):

- *Certification authorities* (CAs) generate certificates and certificate-status information, and

- *Registration authorities* (RAs) verify the identity of users applying for a certificate[65] and authenticate other information to be included in the certificate.

In general, a PKI operates as follows:

1. An entity applies to an RA to request a certificate.

2. The RA verifies the identity of the applicant, and 2) verifies the information to be inserted in the certificate.

3. If the checks made by the RA in step 2 indicate that the information to be inserted in the certificate is valid, then the RA sends the public key and other relevant information to the CA to request that a certificate be generated.

4. Upon receiving the certificate request from the RA, the CA creates a digital certificate, returns the certificate to the RA and deposits the certificate in a repository.

5. When a relying party interacts with another entity that has a public-key certificate, the relying party needs to obtain the other entity's certificate, either directly or from the CA's repository. After acquiring the certificate, the relying entity verifies the signature on the certificate. Assuming that the certificate is "good," then the relying party can proceed safely with its interaction with the certificate's owner.

Most of the interaction involved with using a certificate is transparent to the user. However, a user or a system administrator may be responsible for obtaining and installing a certificate. Thereafter, an application (e.g., a browser) uses the certificate to interact with other entities, and the user may not be aware of these actions. An exception might be when a certificate has expired or been revoked, in which case a message may be displayed to indicate this status.

Certificates expire at a predetermined time unless revoked prior to the expiration date. Certificates can be revoked for a variety of reasons, including the compromise of the private key corresponding to the public key in the certificate, or the owner of the certificate leaving the organization. When a certificate has been revoked, a system will quite often display the certificate-revocation message and perhaps include the reason for the revocation. Depending on the application implementation and the revocation reason, the application could disallow further actions, or could allow the user to indicate whether to ignore the warning and continue operations, or to simply discontinue operations. This warning must not be taken lightly. Ignoring the warning means that the user is accepting the risks associated with doing so. For example, if a warning indicates a compromised

---

[64] SP 800-32, *Introduction to Public Key Technology and the Federal PKI Infrastructure.*

[65] The certificate could be for the user or for a device for which the user is authorized to obtain a certificate.

digital signature certificate, there is a possibility that someone other than the claimed owner of the certificate actually used the private key corresponding to the public key to sign data. Depending on the data, it may not be prudent to ignore the warning. A user should consult with his organization to determine how to respond to this warning.

5.2.3.2 Basic Certificate Verification Process

A PKI consists of at least one CA with its subscribers, as shown in Figure 5. Each of the subscribers (e.g., User 1, User 2 and User 3) obtains a certificate containing their public key and other information, which is signed by their CA. All CA subscribers are provided with the public key of the CA.

As a basic example of how this works, suppose that User 3 signs a document and sends it to User 1, who needs to verify the contents and source of the signed document. This is accomplished as follows:

1. User 1 obtains the certificate containing the public key that corresponds to the private key used to sign the document, i.e., User 1 obtains User 3's certificate. Either User 3 supplies that certificate, or the certificate is obtained from some other source, e.g., the CA.

2. User 1 verifies User 3's certificate using the CA's public key.

3. User 1 then employs the public key in User 3's certificate to verify the signature on the document received from User 3. If the signature is successfully verified, then User 1 knows that User 3 generated the signature, and no unauthorized modifications were made to the document after the signature was generated.

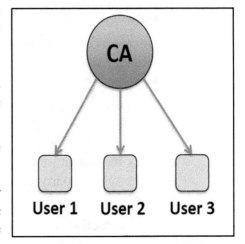

Figure 5: Basic Certificate Verification Example

Note that other more-complicated scenarios exist when users subscribing to different CAs need to interact using CAs that have cross certified by signing a certificate for each other.

5.2.3.3 CA Certificate Policies and Certificate Practice Statements

Each CA has a Certificate Policy and a Certificate Practices Statement. As defined by ITU[66] Recommendation X.509, a Certificate Policy (CP) is "a named set of rules that indicates the applicability of a certificate to a particular community and/or class of application with common security requirements." The CP defines the expectations and requirements of the relying party community that will trust the certificates issued by the CAs using that policy. A CP addresses such issues as key generation and storage;

---

[66] International Telecommunication Union.

certificate generation; key escrow[67] and recovery; certificate status services, including Certificate Revocation List (CRL) generation and distribution; and system management functions, such as security audits, configuration management, and archiving.

A Certification Practice Statement (CPS) describes how a specific CA issues and manages public-key certificates. The CPS is derived from the applicable CP for the community or application in which the CA participates.

A Federal Public Key Infrastructure (FPKI) has been established for use by the Federal Government (see Section 5.2.3.4 for further information).

DRAFT NISTIR 7924[68] identifies a baseline set of security controls and practices to support the secure issuance of certificates. NISTIR 7924 is designed to be used as a template and guide for writing a CP for a specific community, or a CPS for a specific CA.

5.2.3.4   Federal Public Key Infrastructure

A Federal Public Key Infrastructure (FPKI) provides the Federal Government with a common infrastructure to administer digital certificates and public-private key pairs. The network portion of the FPKI (commonly referred to as the "Bridge") consists of "Principal CAs" designated by various agencies. Each CA within the bridge is cross-certified with every other CA within the bridge, thus establishing a conduit for trust relationships among all CAs within the FPKI. Each Principal CA may also be associated with other CAs that are not part of the bridge. For more information about the FPKI, including its certificate policy and certificate practices statement, see http://www.idmanagement.gov/federal-public-key-infrastructure.

5.3   Key Establishment

Key establishment is the means by which keys are generated and provided to the entities that are authorized to use them. An entity may be a person, organization, device or process. Scenarios for which key establishment could be performed include the following:

- A single entity could generate a key (see Section 5.3.1) and use it without providing it to other entities (e.g., for protecting locally stored data),

- A key could be derived from a key that is already shared between two or more entities (see Section 5.3.2),

- Two entities could generate a key using contributions (i.e., data) from each entity using an automated protocol that incorporates a key-agreement scheme (see Section 5.3.3), or

---

[67] Saving a key or information that allows the key to be reconstructed so that the key can be recovered if ever needed (e.g., because of being lost or corrupted).

[68] NISTIR 7924, *Reference Certificate Policy (Second Draft)*.

- A single entity could generate a key and provide it to one or more other entities, either by a manual means (e.g., a courier or a face-to-face meeting, with the key in either printed or electronic form, such as on a flash drive) or using automated protocols that incorporate a key-transport scheme (see Sections 5.3.4 and 5.3.5).

5.3.1 Key Generation

Cryptographic keys are required by most cryptographic algorithms, the exception being hash functions when not used as a component of another cryptographic process (e.g., HMAC). SP 800-133[69] discusses the generation of the keys to be used with the **approved** cryptographic algorithms.

All keys must be based directly or indirectly on the output of an **approved** Random Bit Generator (RBG) and must be generated within FIPS 140-compliant cryptographic modules (see FIPS 140). Any random value required by the module must be generated within a cryptographic module.

SP 800-133 provides guidance on generating a key directly from an RBG, and references other publications for additional information required for the generation of keys for specific algorithms:

- FIPS 186 provides rules for the generation of the key pairs to be used for the generation of digital signatures,

- SP 800-108 provides methods for the generation of keys from an already-shared key (see Section 5.3.2),

- SP 800-56A specifies the rules for the generation of key pairs for Diffie-Hellman and MQV key-agreement schemes (see Section 5.3.3),

- SP 800-56B specifies the rules for the generation of key pairs for RSA key-agreement and key-transport schemes (see Sections 5.3.3 and 5.3.4, respectively), and

- SP 800-132 specifies the rules for the generation of keys from passwords (see Section 5.3.6).

5.3.2 Key Derivation

Key derivation is concerned with the generation of a key from secret information, although non-secret information may also be used in the generation process in addition to the secret information. Typically, the secret information is shared among entities that need to derive the same key for subsequent interactions. The secret information could be a key that is already shared between the entities (i.e., a pre-shared key), or could be a shared secret that is derived during a key-agreement scheme (see Section 5.3.3).

SP 800-108[70] specifies several key-derivation functions that use pre-shared keys. A pre-shared key could have been

---

[69] SP 800-133, *Recommendation for Cryptographic Key Generation.*

[70] SP 800-108, *Recommendation for Key Derivation Using Pseudorandom Functions.*

- Generated by one entity and provided to one or more other entities by some manual means (e.g., a courier or face-to-face meeting),

- Agreed upon by the entities using an automated key-agreement scheme (see Section 5.3.3), or

- Generated by one entity and provided to another entity using an automated key-transport scheme (see Sections 5.3.4 and 5.3.5).

SP 800-56A, SP 800-56B and SP 800-56C[71] provide methods for deriving keys from the shared secrets generated during key agreement (see Section 5.3.3). SP 800-56A and SP 800-56 B specify two key-derivation methods for this purpose, and refer to SP 800-56C and SP 800-135[72] for additional **approved** methods[73].

5.3.3 Key Agreement

Key agreement is a key-establishment procedure in which the resultant keying material is a function of information contributed by all participants in the key-agreement process so that no participant can predetermine the value of the resulting keying material independently of the contributions of the other participants. Key agreement is usually performed using automated protocols.

SP 800-56A and SP 800-56B provide several automated pair-wise key-agreement schemes, i.e., key-agreement schemes involving two parties. For each scheme, a shared secret is generated, and keying material is derived from the shared secret using a key-derivation method specified or approved by reference in SP 800-56A, SP 800-56B or SP 800-56C.

SP 800-56A and SP 800-56B include variations of key-agreement schemes, differing in the number of keys used and whether the keys are long term (i.e., static) or an ephemeral value (e.g., a nonce or a short-term key pair). The key-agreement schemes have two participating entities: an initiator and a responder.

---

[71] SP 800-56C, *Recommendation for Key Derivation through Extraction-then-Expansion.*

[72] SP 800-135, *Recommendation for Existing Application-Specific Key Derivation Functions.*

[73] Note that a modification is in progress to move the KDF specifications and references in SP 800-56A and SP 800-56B to SP 800-56C.

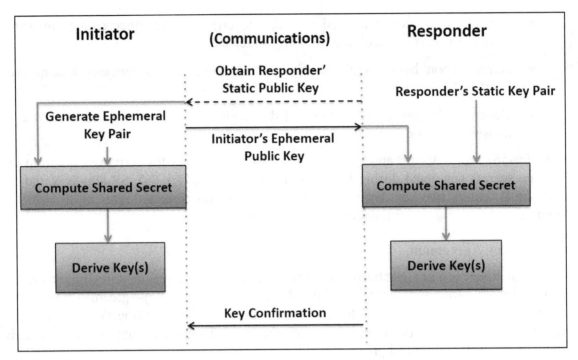

Figure 6: Key Agreement Example

Figure 6 provides an example of a key-agreement scheme where the responder uses a static key pair during the scheme, and the initiator uses an ephemeral key pair. Note that other key-agreement schemes may use other arrangements of key pairs (e.g., each party could use a static key pair or each party could use an ephemeral key pair). In the example provided in the figure above, the responder's private key is retained by the responder (who is the owner of the key pair), but the responder's public key may be provided to anyone. In this example, the public key is provided to the initiator:

1. The initiator obtains the responder's public key (e.g., from a CA or directly from the responder); for this scheme, this public key is the responder's contribution to the key-agreement process.

2. The initiator then generates a short-term key pair (i.e., an ephemeral key pair), and sends the ephemeral public key to the responder, retaining the ephemeral private key. The ephemeral public key is the initiator's contribution to the key-agreement process for this scheme.

3. Both parties use their own key pair and the other party's public key to generate a shared secret.

4. Both parties then use their copy of the shared secret to derive one or more keys that are (hopefully) identical.

Key confirmation is an optional, but highly recommended, step that provides assurance that both parties now have the same (identical) key(s), and is shown in Figure 6 for the case that the initiator receives key confirmation from the responder. See SP 800-56A and SP 800-56B for further information.

SP 800-56A specifies Diffie-Hellman (DH) and MQV key-agreement schemes using finite field or elliptic curve mathematics and asymmetric key pairs to generate the shared secret, and SP 800-56B specifies two RSA key-agreement schemes. SP 800-56A and SP 800-56B also provide an analysis of the merits of each key-agreement scheme.

5.3.4 Key Transport

Key transport is a method whereby one party (the sender) generates a key and distributes it to one or more other parties (the receiver(s)). Key transport could be accomplished using manual methods (e.g., using a courier) or performed using automated protocols. SP 800-56A and SP 800-56B provide automated pair-wise key-transport schemes, and an analysis of the merits of each key-transport scheme.

5.3.4.1 SP 800-56A Key Transport

SP 800-56A specifies a key-transport method whereby a key-establishment transaction includes both a key-agreement process and a key-wrapping process. Key wrapping is a process that provides both confidentiality and integrity protection for keying material using a symmetric-key algorithm (see Section 5.3.5 for further information about key wrapping).

During the transaction, the key generated during the key-agreement part of the transaction is used as a key-wrapping key with a symmetric-key algorithm (e.g., AES) by the sending party to wrap a key to be sent to the other party (the receiver). Note that the sender can be either the initiator or the responder in the key-agreement process.

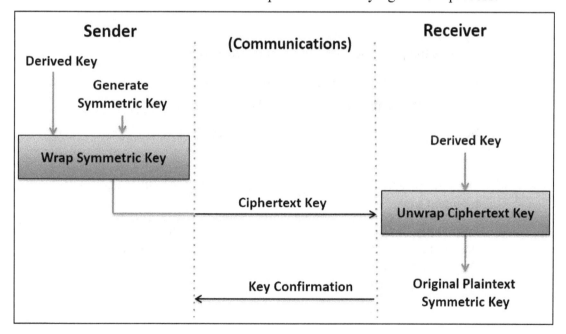

Figure 7: SP 800-56A Key Transport Example

Figure 7 illustrates the key transport process that follows the key-agreement discussed in Section 5.3.3 and shown in Figure 6. After the key-agreement part of the transaction, the initiator and responder share a symmetric key-wrapping key, which is then used as follows:

The sender:

1. Generates (or otherwise obtains) a symmetric key to be transported (note that the sender could have been either the initiator or the responder in the key-agreement part of the transaction),

2. Wraps the symmetric key from step 1 using the key-wrapping key, and

3. Sends the resulting ciphertext (i.e., the wrapped key) to the intended receiver.

The receiver:

4. Unwraps the ciphertext using his copy of the key-wrapping key to obtain the original plaintext symmetric key, and

5. Optionally performs key confirmation; although this step is optional, it is highly recommended to provide assurance that both parties now have the same symmetric key.

5.3.4.2 SP 800-56B Key Transport

SP 800-56B specifies two very different methods for transporting keys whereby the sender uses the receiver's public key to securely transport keying material to the receiver.

Figure 8 provides a simplified example of one of the key-transport methods in SP 800-56B. In both methods, the receiver must have a key pair that is used during a key-transport transaction. In the example shown in the figure, key transport is accomplished as follows.

The sender:

1. Obtains the public key of the intended receiver,

2. Generates a symmetric key to be transported,

3. Encrypts the symmetric key using the receiver's public key, and

4. Sends the resulting ciphertext key to the receiver.

The receiver:

5. Uses his private key to decrypt the ciphertext key, thus obtaining the original plaintext key.

6. Optionally performs key confirmation; although this step is optional, it is highly recommended to provide assurance that both parties now have the same symmetric key.

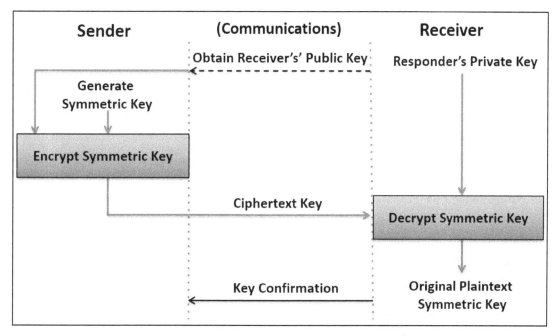

Figure 8: SP 800-56B Key Transport Example

5.3.5   Key Wrapping

Key wrapping is a method used to provide confidentiality and integrity protection to keys (and possibly other information) using a symmetric key-wrapping key that is known by both the sender and receiver, and a symmetric-key block cipher algorithm. The wrapped keying material can then be stored or transmitted (i.e., transported) securely. Unwrapping the keying material requires the use of the same algorithm and key-wrapping key that was used during the original wrapping process.

Key wrapping differs from simple encryption in that the wrapping process includes an integrity feature. During the unwrapping process, this integrity feature is used to detect accidental or intentional modifications to the wrapped keying material.

Three methods have been specified in SP 800-38F[74] for key wrapping, and other SP 800-38 modes (or combination of modes) that that can also be used for key wrapping are also **approved** in SP 800-38F. Depending on the method or mode, either AES or TDEA can be used.

5.3.6   Derivation of a Key from a Password

Keys can be derived from passwords. Due to the ease of guessing most passwords, keys derived in this manner are not suitable to be used for most applications. However, SP 800-132[75] specifies a family of functions that can be used to derive keying material from

---

[74] SP 800-38F, *Recommendation for Block Cipher Modes of Operation: Methods for Key Wrapping.*

[75] SP 800-132, *Recommendation for Password-Based Key Derivation Part 1: Storage Applications.*

a password[76] for electronic storage applications (e.g., when encrypting an entire disk drive).

5.4   Key Management Issues

A number of issues need to be addressed for selecting and using a CKMS.

5.4.1   Manual vs. Automated Key Establishment

As discussed in Sections 5.3 and 5.3.4, keys can be established between entities either manually or using automated methods. In many cases, a hybrid approach is used in which an entity generates and manually distributes one or more keys to other entities, and thereafter these keys are used to establish other keys (see SP 800-56A and SP 800-56B).

The number of keys to be manually distributed depends on the type of cryptography to be used (i.e., symmetric or asymmetric methods) and must be considered when selecting the capabilities required of a CKMS.

5.4.2   Selecting and Operating a CKMS

A CKMS could be designed, implemented and operated by the organization that will use it. Or, the organization could operate a CKMS procured from a vendor. Or, an organization could procure the services of a third party that procures a CKMS from a vendor. Whichever choice is made, the organization needs to make sure that the CKMS that is used provides the protections that are required for the organization's information. SP 800-130 and SP 800-152 discuss the considerations that need to be addressed by the federal organization, including the scalability of the CKMS, and the metadata to be associated with the keys.

5.4.3   Storing and Protecting Keys

Keys can be stored in a number of places and protected in a variety of ways. They could be stored in a safe. They could be present only in a validated cryptographic module where the module itself might adequately protect the keys, depending on its design. Keys could also be stored on electronic media, such as a flash drive; in this case, a key may need to be encrypted or split into key components so that no single person can determine what the key is. These issues need to be addressed for operational keys.

Certain keys may need to be backed up so that if an operational key is inadvertently lost or modified, it can be recovered and operations resumed. Some keys may also need to be archived for long-term storage (e.g., because of legal requirements or to decrypt archived data). A key-recovery capability is needed whenever keys are backed up or archived. This capability needs to be designed so that the keys can be recovered in an acceptable amount of time and only by those entities authorized to do so; see SP 800-57, Part 1 for more information about key backup, key archiving and key recovery.

---

[76] Note that this publication considers a passphrase to be a password.

5.4.4 Cryptoperiods

A cryptoperiod is the time span during which a specific key is authorized for use. A cryptoperiod for a key is assigned for a number of reasons, including limiting the amount of exposure of encrypted data if a single key is compromised. Cryptoperiods are usually assigned for a carefully considered period of time or by the maximum amount of data protected by the key. Tradeoffs associated with the determination of a cryptoperiod involve the risks and consequences of exposure. Section 5.3 of SP 800-57, Part 1 provides a more detailed discussion of the need for establishing cryptoperiods, the factors to be considered when deciding on a suitable cryptoperiod and some suggestions for the length of cryptoperiods.

5.4.5 Use Validated Algorithms and Cryptographic Modules

Cryptographic algorithms must be validated and implemented in FIPS 140-validated cryptographic modules. Every IT product available makes a claim as to functionality and/or offered security. When protecting sensitive data, a minimum level of assurance is needed that a product's stated security claim is valid. There are also legislative restrictions regarding certain types of technology, such as cryptography, that require federal agencies to use only tested and validated products.

Federal agencies, private industry, and the public rely on cryptography for the protection of information and communications used in electronic commerce, the critical infrastructure, and other application areas. At the core of all products offering cryptographic services is the cryptographic module. Cryptographic modules, which contain cryptographic algorithms, are used in products and systems to provide security services such as confidentiality, integrity, and authentication. Although cryptography is used to provide security, weaknesses such as poor design or weak algorithms can render the product insecure and place highly sensitive information at risk. Adequate testing and validation of the cryptographic module and its underlying cryptographic algorithms against established standards is essential to provide security assurance.

NIST has established programs to validate the implementation of the **approved** cryptographic algorithms and the cryptographic modules in which they are used: the Cryptographic Algorithm Validation Program (CAVP) and the Cryptographic Module Validation Program (CMVP). Information about the CAVP is available at http://csrc.nist.gov/groups/STM/cavp/, while information about the CMVP is available at http://csrc.nist.gov/groups/STM/cmvp/.

Also, see Section 5.1.2 in this document for a discussion of the security requirements for cryptographic modules.

5.4.6 Control of Keying Material

The access to keys needs to be controlled. A key should only be accessible by an authorized entity, and only for the purpose for which it is authorized. For example, a key designated for key transport must not be used for the generation or verification of digital signatures.

The proliferation of keys also needs to be controlled. While it is often convenient to make copies of keys, these extra copies need to be accounted for. If a key is compromised, that key and all its copies may need to be destroyed to prevent subsequent unauthorized use. For example, if a private key used for the generation of a digital signature is compromised, and a copy of the key still exists after the original copy was destroyed, then there is a possibility that the copy could be used to generate unauthorized digital signatures at a later time.

Users must be provided with a list of responsibilities and liabilities, and each user should sign a statement acknowledging these concerns before receiving a key. Users must be made aware of their unique responsibilities, especially regarding the significance of a key compromise or loss. Users must be able to store their secret and private keys securely, so that no intruder can access them, yet the keys must be readily accessible for legitimate use.

5.4.7 Compromises

It is imperative to have a plan for handling the compromise or suspected compromise of keys, particularly those used and managed at a central site (e.g., the keys used by a CA to sign certificates); this should be established before the system becomes operational. A compromise-recovery plan should address what actions will be taken with compromised system software and hardware, CA keys, user keys, previously generated signatures, encrypted data, etc. SP 800-57, Part 1 includes discussions of the effects of a key compromise, measures for minimizing the likelihood or consequences of a key compromise, and what should be considered in developing a compromise-recovery plan.

If someone's private or secret key is lost or compromised, other users must be made aware of this, so that they will no longer initiate the protection of data using a compromised key, or accept data protected with a compromised key without assessing and accepting the risk of doing so. This notification is often accomplished using CRLs or Compromised Key Lists (CKLs); see SP 800-57, Part 1 for discussions.

In some cases, a key and all copies of the key should be destroyed immediately upon the detection of a key compromise. For example, a private key used for the generation of digital signatures should be immediately destroyed. However, the corresponding public key may need to remain available for verifying the signatures that were previously generated using the compromised private key. Note that there is a risk associated with accepting these signatures.

5.4.8 Accountability and Auditing

Accountability involves the identification of those entities that have access to or control of cryptographic keys throughout their lifecycles. Accountability can be an effective tool to help prevent key compromises and to reduce the impact of compromises when they are detected. Accountability 1) aids in the determination of when a compromise could have occurred and what individuals could have been involved, 2) discourages key compromise because users know their access to the key is known, and 3) is useful in determining where the key was used and what data or other keys were protected by a compromised key, and therefore, may also be compromised.

Auditing is another mechanism used for the detection of and recovery from key compromises. Auditing includes reviewing the actions of humans that use, operate and maintain systems, looking for unusual events that may indicate inappropriate actions by the humans or processes using a key management system.

SECTION 6: OTHER ISSUES

The use of cryptography should not be undertaken without a thorough risk analysis, and a determination of the sensitivity of the information to be protected and the security controls to be used (see SP 800-175A and SP 800-53). After performing a risk assessment and determining the sensitivity level of the information to be protected (Low, Moderate or High) and the security controls to be used, a number of issues need to be addressed to ensure that cryptography is used properly.

This section identifies issues to be addressed after determining that cryptography is required.

6.1 Required Security Strength

The minimum security strength is determined by the sensitivity level of the information (see FIPS 199). SP 800-152 requires a security strength of at least 112 bits for the protection of Low-impact information, 128 bits for Moderate-impact information, and 192 bits for High-impact information. The required security strength can then be used to determine the algorithm and key size to be used. Section 5.6 of SP 800-57, Part 1 provides tables for selecting appropriate algorithms and key sizes.

Many applications require the use of several different cryptographic algorithms. Ideally, these algorithms would all offer the same security strength, but this may not always be the case for performance, availability and interoperability reasons. When algorithms of different strengths are used together to protect data, the security provided by the combination of algorithms is the strength associated with the algorithm with the lowest security strength (see Section 5.6 of SP 800-57, Part 1). For example, RSA with 2048-bit keys can support a security strength of 112 bits, but is often used with SHA-256, which can support a security strength of 128 bits. When the combination is used to generate a digital signature, the signature can only provide a security strength of 112 bits – the lesser strength offered by the two algorithms.

Approved combinations of algorithms (called cipher suites) for some of the protocols are provided in SP 800-57, Part 3 (for S/MIME) and SP 800-52 (for TLS).

6.2   Interoperability

Interoperability is the ability of one entity to communicate with another entity, whether the entities are people, devices or processes. In order to communicate, the entities must have:

- A communications channel (e.g., the Internet) and the same communications protocol (e.g., TLS), and

- Policies that allow the entities to communicate.

In order to communicate securely, the entities must also have:

- Trust that each entity will enforce its own policies.

- Interoperable cryptographic capabilities as discussed in Section 4, and

- Share appropriate keying material that has been established securely (see Section 5.3).

For example, if entities A and B are in two different organizations, and

- Each organization has a policy that allows the entities to communicate,

- Each entity trusts that the other entity will enforce its own policies,

- There is a TLS capability that can be used for communication,

- Each entity can encrypt and decrypt information using AES with a 128-bit key and establish keys using 3072-bit RSA key transport (see Section 5.3.4), and

- One of the entities can generate a 128-bit AES key and act as the sender in the key-transport scheme, and the other entity has a 3072-bit RSA key pair and can act as the receiver (see Section 5.3.4.2 for a discussion on key transport),

then the two entities have a secure and interoperable communication channel that can be used to establish a 128-bit key for encrypting information using AES. In this case, the security strength that can be provided by an encryption operation using AES is 128 bits, since both 3072-bit RSA and AES-128 are rated at a security strength of 128 bits (see Section 6.1).

6.3 When Algorithms are No Longer Approved

In the case that an algorithm is **no longer approved** for providing adequate protection (e.g., the algorithm may have been "broken"), a risk assessment needs to be performed to determine whether the information should be re-protected using an **approved** algorithm and key size that will protect the information for the remainder of its security life. See Section 5.6.4 for SP 800-57, Part 1 for additional discussion.

6.4 Registration Authorities (RAs)

As discussed in Section 5.2.3.1, an RA verifies the identity of users applying for a certificate and authenticates other information to be included in a certificate generated by a Certification Authority (CA). The correctness of this information is the linchpin on which the security of using certificates is based. Once this information is verified, the appropriate information is submitted to a CA for certificate generation using a signed certification request. The CA must deem the RA as trustworthy, e.g.,

- Appropriate identification is provided by an entity requesting a certificate and is fully checked by the RA;

- Information submitted for inclusion in the certificate is checked for validity (e.g., that the public key is valid, and the private key is in the possession of the claimed owner); and

- The RA provides adequate protection for the private key used to sign the certification request.

6.5   Cross Certification

Cross certification is the establishment of a trust relationship between two Certification Authorities (CAs) through the signing of each other's public key in a certificate referred to as a "cross-certificate." Cross-certificates provide a means to create a chain of trust from a single, trusted, root CA to multiple other CAs so that subscribers in one CA domain can interact safely with subscribers in other CA domains (e.g., the subscriber in one CA domain has assurance of the identity of the subscriber in the other domain and assurance of the accurateness of the other information provided by his certificate).

Cross certification should only be performed when each CA examines the other CA's policies, finds them acceptable and trusts that CA to operate in accordance with those policies.

Appendix A: References

The following FIPS and NIST Special Publications (SP) apply to the use of cryptography in the Federal Government.

All publications are available at http://csrc.nist.gov/publications.

FIPS 140	Federal Information Processing Standard 140-2, *Security Requirements for Cryptographic Modules*, May 25, 2001 (updated December 3, 2002 (Change Notice 2)). http://csrc.nist.gov/publications/fips/fips140-2/fips1402.pdf [accessed 8/18/16]. FIPS 140-2 specifies the requirements that must be met by cryptographic modules protecting U.S. Government information. The standard provides four increasing, qualitative levels of security. The security requirements cover areas related to the secure design and implementation of a cryptographic module.
FIPS 180	Federal Information Processing Standard 180-4, *Secure Hash Standard (SHS)*, August 2015. http://dx.doi.org/10.6028/NIST.FIPS.180-4 FIPS 180-4 specifies seven cryptographic hash algorithms: SHA-1, SHA-224, SHA-256, SHA-384, SHA-512, SHA-512/224 and SHA-512/256.
FIPS 185	Federal Information Processing Standard 185, *Escrowed Encryption Standard*, February 9, 1994 [withdrawn October 19, 2015]. http://csrc.nist.gov/publications/fips/fips185/fips185.pdf [accessed 8/18/16]. FIPS 185 specified the use of an encryption/decryption algorithm and a Law Enforcement Access Field (LEAF) creation method that could be implemented in electronic devices and used for protecting government telecommunications when such protection was desired. The algorithm and the LEAF creation method were classified. The LEAF was intended for use in a key escrow system that provided for the decryption of telecommunications when access to the telecommunications was lawfully authorized.
FIPS 186	Federal Information Processing Standard 186-4, *Digital Signature Standard (DSS)*, July 2013. http://dx.doi.org/10.6028/NIST.FIPS.180-4 FIPS 186-4 specifies a suite of algorithms that can be used to generate a digital signature: DSA, ECDSA and RSA. This Standard includes methods for the generation of digital signatures, methods for the generation of domain parameters (for DSA and ECDSA), and methods for the generation of key pairs, and requires certain

	assurances for using digital signatures: assurance of domain-parameter validity (DSA and ECDSA), and assurance of public-key validity and assurance of private-key possession for all three algorithms.
FIPS 197	Federal Information Processing Standard 197, *Advanced Encryption Standard (AES)*, November 26, 2001. http://csrc.nist.gov/publications/fips/fips197/fips-197.pdf [accessed 8/18/16]. FIPS 197 specifies a symmetric key block cipher algorithm. The Standard supports key sizes of 128, 192, and 256 bits and a block size of 128 bits.
FIPS 198	Federal Information Processing Standard 198-1, *Keyed-Hash Message Authentication Code (HMAC)*, July 2008. http://csrc.nist.gov/publications/fips/fips198-1/FIPS-198-1_final.pdf [accessed 8/18/16]. FIPS 198-1 defines a message authentication code (MAC) that uses a cryptographic hash function in conjunction with a secret key for the calculation and verification of the MACs.
FIPS 199	Federal Information Processing Standard 199, *Standards for Security Categorization of Federal Information and Information Systems,* February 2004. http://csrc.nist.gov/publications/fips/fips199/FIPS-PUB-199-final.pdf [accessed 8/18/16]. FIPS 199 establishes security categories for both information and information systems. The security categories are based on the potential impact on an organization if certain events occur that jeopardize the information and information systems needed by the organization to accomplish its assigned mission, protect its assets, fulfill its legal responsibilities, maintain its day-to-day functions, and protect individuals.
FIPS 202	Federal Information Processing Standard 202, *SHA-3 Standard: Permutation-Based Hash and Extendable-Output Functions*, August 2015. http://dx.doi.org/10.6028/NIST.FIPS.202 FIPS 202 specifies SHA3-224, SHA3-256, SHA3-384 and SHA3-512. This FIPS also specifies two extendable-output functions (SHAKE128 and SHAKE256), which are not, in themselves, considered to be hash functions.

SP 800-22	Special Publication 800-22 Revision 1a, *A Statistical Test Suite for Random and Pseudorandom Number Generators for Cryptographic Applications*, April 2010. http://dx.doi.org/10.6028/NIST.SP.800-22r1a SP 800-22 discusses some aspects of selecting and testing random and pseudorandom number generators for providing random numbers that are indistinguishable from truly random output.
SP 800-32	Special Publication 800-32, *Introduction to Public Key Technology and the Federal PKI Infrastructure*, February 26, 2001. http://dx.doi.org/10.6028/NIST.SP.800-32 SP 800-32 was developed to assist agency decision-makers in determining if a PKI is appropriate for their agency, and how PKI services can be deployed most effectively within a Federal agency. It is intended to provide an overview of PKI functions and their applications.
SP 800-38	A series of publications specifying modes of operation for block cipher algorithms.
SP 800-38A	Special Publication 800-38A, *Recommendation for Block Cipher Modes of Operation: Methods and Techniques*, December 2001. http://dx.doi.org/10.6028/NIST.SP.800-38A SP 800-38A defines five confidentiality modes of operation for use with an underlying symmetric key block cipher algorithm: Electronic Codebook (ECB), Cipher Block Chaining (CBC), Cipher Feedback (CFB), Output Feedback (OFB), and Counter (CTR). Used with an **approved** underlying block cipher algorithm (i.e., AES and TDEA), these modes can provide cryptographic protection for sensitive computer data.
SP 800-38B	Special Publication 800-38B, *Recommendation for Block Cipher Modes of Operation: the CMAC Mode for Authentication*, May 2005. http://dx.doi.org/10.6028/NIST.SP.800-38B SP 800-38B specifies a message authentication code (MAC) algorithm based on a symmetric key block cipher (i.e., AES or TDEA). This block cipher-based MAC algorithm, called CMAC, may be used to provide assurance of the source and integrity of binary data.

SP 800-38C	Special Publication 800-38C, *Recommendation for Block Cipher Modes of Operation: the CCM Mode for Authentication and Confidentiality*, May 2004 (updated July 20, 2007).
	http://dx.doi.org/10.6028/NIST.SP.800-38C
	SP 800-38C defines a mode of operation, called CCM, for a symmetric-key block cipher algorithm with a 128-bit block size (i.e., AES). CCM may be used to provide assurance of the confidentiality and the authenticity of computer data by combining the techniques of the Counter (CTR) mode specified in SP 800-38A, and the Cipher Block Chaining-Message Authentication Code (CBC-MAC) algorithm (specified in SP 800-90B, but **not** currently approved for general use).
SP 800-38D	Special Publication 800-38D, *Recommendation for Block Cipher Modes of Operation: Galois/Counter Mode (GCM) and GMAC*, November 2007.
	http://dx.doi.org/10.6028/NIST.SP.800-38D
	SP 800-38D specifies the Galois/Counter Mode (GCM), an algorithm for authenticated encryption with associated data, and its specialization, GMAC, for generating a message authentication code (MAC) on data that is not encrypted. GCM and GMAC are modes of operation for an underlying, **approved** symmetric-key block cipher with a 128-bit block size (i.e., AES).
SP 800-38E	Special Publication 800-38E, *Recommendation for Block Cipher Modes of Operation: the XTS-AES Mode for Confidentiality on Storage Devices*, January 2010.
	http://dx.doi.org/10.6028/NIST.SP.800-38E
	SP 800-38E approves the XTS-AES mode of the AES algorithm by reference to IEEE 1619, subject to one additional requirement, as an option for protecting the confidentiality of data on storage devices. The mode does not provide authentication of the data or its source.

SP 800-38F	Special Publication 800-38F, *Recommendation for Block Cipher Modes of Operation: Methods for Key Wrapping*, December 2012. http://dx.doi.org/10.6028/NIST.SP.800-38F SP 800-38F describes cryptographic methods that are approved for key wrapping. In addition to approving existing methods, this publication specifies two new, deterministic authenticated-encryption modes of operation of the Advanced Encryption Standard (AES) algorithm: the AES Key Wrap (KW) mode and the AES Key Wrap with Padding (KWP) mode. An analogous mode with the Triple Data Encryption Algorithm (TDEA) as the underlying block cipher, called TKW, is also specified to support legacy applications.
SP 800-38G	Special Publication 800-38G, *Recommendation for Block Cipher Modes of Operation: Methods for Format-Preserving Encryption*, March 2016. http://dx.doi.org/10.6028/NIST.SP.800-38G SP 800-38G specifies methods for format-preserving encryption, called FF1 and FF3. Each of these methods is a mode of operation of the AES algorithm, which is used to construct a round function within the Feistel structure for encryption.
SP 800-52	Special Publication 800-52 Revision 1, *Guidelines for the Selection, Configuration, and Use of Transport Layer Security (TLS) Implementations*, April 2014. http://dx.doi.org/10.6028/NIST.SP.800-52r1 Transport Layer Security (TLS) provides mechanisms to protect sensitive data during electronic dissemination across the Internet. SP 800-52 provides guidance about the selection and configuration of TLS protocol implementations, while making effective use of Federal Information Processing Standards (FIPS) and NIST-recommended cryptographic algorithms (specified in SPs), and requires that TLS 1.1 be configured with FIPS-based cipher suites as the minimum appropriate secure transport protocol. This publication also identifies TLS extensions for which mandatory support must be provided and identifies other recommended extensions.
SP 800-53	Special Publication 800-53 Revision 4, *Security and Privacy Controls for Federal Information Systems and Organizations*, April 2013 (updated January 22, 2015). http://dx.doi.org/10.6028/NIST.SP.800-53r4 SP 800-53 provides a catalog of security and privacy controls for federal information systems and organizations, and a process for selecting controls to protect organizational operations (including

	mission, functions, image, and reputation), organizational assets, individuals, other organizations, and the Nation from a diverse set of threats, including hostile cyber attacks, natural disasters, structural failures, and human errors.
SP 800-56A	Special Publication 800-56A Revision 2, *Recommendation for Pair-Wise Key-Establishment Schemes Using Discrete Logarithm Cryptography*, May 2013. http://dx.doi.org/10.6028/NIST.SP.800-56Ar2 SP 800-56A specifies key-establishment schemes based on the discrete logarithm problem over finite fields and elliptic curves, including several variations of Diffie-Hellman and Menezes-Qu-Vanstone (MQV) key-establishment schemes.
SP 800-56B	Special Publication 800-56B Revision 1, *Recommendation for Pair-Wise Key-Establishment Schemes Using Integer Factorization Cryptography*, September 2014. http://dx.doi.org/10.6028/NIST.SP.800-56Br1 SP 800-56B specifies key-establishment schemes using integer-factorization cryptography (RSA). Both key transport and key-agreement schemes are specified.
SP 800-56C	Special Publication 800-56C, *Recommendation for Key Derivation through Extraction-then-Expansion*, November 2011. http://dx.doi.org/10.6028/NIST.SP.800-56C SP 800-56C specifies techniques for the derivation of keying material from a shared secret established during a key-establishment scheme defined in SP 800-56A or SP 800-56B through an extraction-then-expansion procedure.
SP 800-57, Part 1	Special Publication 800-57, Part 1 Revision 4, *Recommendation for Key Management, Part 1: General*, January 2016. http://dx.doi.org/10.6028/NIST.SP.800-57pt1r4 Part 1 of SP 800-57 provides general guidance and best practices for the management of cryptographic keying material. It focuses on issues involving the management of cryptographic keys: their generation, use, and eventual destruction. Related topics, such as algorithm selection and appropriate key size, cryptographic policy, and cryptographic module selection, are also included.

SP 800-57, Part 2	Special Publication 800-57, Part 2, *Recommendation for Key Management, Part 2: Best Practices for Key Management Organization*, August 2005. http://dx.doi.org/10.6028/NIST.SP.800-57p2 Part 2 of SP 800-57 provides guidance on policy and security planning requirements for U.S. government agencies. This part of SP 800-57 contains a generic key-management infrastructure, guidance for the development of organizational key-management policy statements and key-management practices statements, an identification of key-management information that needs to be incorporated into security plans for general support systems and major applications that employ cryptography, and an identification of key-management information that needs to be documented for all Federal applications of cryptography.
SP 800-57, Part 3	Special Publication 800-57, Part 3 Revision 1, *Recommendation for Key Management, Part 3: Application-Specific Key Management Guidance*, January 2015. http://dx.doi.org/10.6028/NIST.SP.800-57pt3r1 Part 3 of SP 800-57 addresses the key-management issues associated with currently available cryptographic mechanisms, such as the Public Key infrastructure (PKI), Internet Protocol Security (IPsec), the Transport Layer Security protocol (TLS), Secure/Multipart Internet Mail Extensions (S/MIME), Kerberos, Over-the-Air Rekeying (OTAR), Domain Name System Security Extensions (DNSSEC), Encrypted File Systems and the Secure Shell (SSH) protocol.
SP 800-67	Special Publication 800-67 Revision 1, *Recommendation for the Triple Data Encryption Algorithm (TDEA) Block Cipher*, January 2012. http://dx.doi.org/10.6028/NIST.SP.800-67r1 SP 800-67 specifies the Triple Data Encryption Algorithm (TDEA), including its primary component cryptographic engine, the Data Encryption Algorithm (DEA).
SP 800-89	Special Publication 800-89, *Recommendation for Obtaining Assurances for Digital Signature Applications*, November 2006. http://dx.doi.org/10.6028/NIST.SP.800-89 Entities participating in the generation or verification of digital signatures depend on the authenticity of the process. SP 800-89 specifies methods for obtaining the assurances necessary for valid digital signatures: assurance of domain parameter validity, assurance

	of public key validity, assurance that the key-pair owner actually possesses the private key, and assurance of the identity of the key pair owner.
SP 800-90A	Special Publication 800-90A Revision 1, *Recommendation for Random Number Generation Using Deterministic Random Bit Generators*, June 2015.
	http://dx.doi.org/10.6028/NIST.SP.800-90Ar1
	SP 800-90A specifies DRBG mechanisms for the generation of random bits using deterministic methods. The methods provided are based on either hash functions or block cipher algorithms and are designed to support selected security strengths. DRBGs must be initialized from a randomness source that provides sufficient entropy for the security strength to be supported by the DRBG.
SP 800-90B	Special Publication 800-90B (Draft), *Recommendation for the Entropy Sources Used for Random Bit Generation*, January 2016.
	http://csrc.nist.gov/publications/PubsSPs.html#800-90B [accessed 8/18/16].
	SP 800-90B specifies the design principles and requirements for the entropy sources used by Random Bit Generators, including health tests to determine that the entropy source has not failed and tests for the validation of entropy sources.
SP 800-90C	Special Publication 800-90C (Draft), *Recommendation for Random Bit Generator (RBG) Constructions*, April 2016.
	http://csrc.nist.gov/publications/PubsSPs.html#800-90C [accessed 8/18/16].
	SP 800-90C specifies constructions for the implementation of random bit generators (RBGs). An RBG may be a deterministic random bit generator (DRBG) or a non-deterministic random bit generator (NRBG). The constructed RBGs consist of DRBG mechanisms as specified SP 800-90A and entropy sources as specified in SP 800-90B.

SP 800-102	Special Publication 800-102, *Recommendation for Digital Signature Timeliness*, September 2009.
	http://dx.doi.org/10.6028/NIST.SP.800-102
	Establishing the time when a digital signature was generated is often a critical consideration. A signed message that includes the (purported) signing time provides no assurance that the private key was used to sign the message at that time unless the accuracy of the time can be trusted. With the appropriate use of digital signature-based timestamps from a Trusted Timestamp Authority and/or verifier-supplied data that is included in the signed message, the signer can provide some level of assurance about the time that the message was signed.
SP 800-106	Special Publication 800-106, *Randomized Hashing for Digital Signatures*, February 2009.
	http://dx.doi.org/10.6028/NIST.SP.800-106
	NIST-approved digital signature algorithms require the use of an **approved** cryptographic hash function in the generation and verification of signatures. SP 800-106 specifies a method to enhance the security of the cryptographic hash functions used in digital signature applications by randomizing the messages that are signed.
SP 800-107	Special Publication 800-107 Revision 1, *Recommendation for Applications Using Approved Hash Algorithms*, August 2012.
	http://dx.doi.org/10.6028/NIST.SP.800-107r1
	Hash functions that compute a fixed-length message digest from arbitrary length messages are widely used for many purposes in information security. SP 800-107 provides security guidelines for achieving the required or desired security strengths when using cryptographic applications that employ the approved hash functions specified in FIPS 180. These include functions such as digital signatures, Keyed-hash Message Authentication Codes (HMACs) and Hashed-based Key Derivation Functions (hash-based KDFs).
SP 800-108	Special Publication 800-108, *Recommendation for Key Derivation Using Pseudorandom Functions (Revised)*, October 2009.
	http://dx.doi.org/10.6028/NIST.SP.800-108
	SP 800-108 specifies techniques for the derivation of additional keying material from a secret key (i.e., a key-derivation key) using pseudorandom functions. The key-derivation key may have been either established through a key-establishment scheme or shared through some other manner (e.g., a manual key distribution).

SP 800-130	Special Publication 800-130, *A Framework for Designing Cryptographic Key Management Systems*, August 2013. http://dx.doi.org/10.6028/NIST.SP.800-130 SP 800-130 contains topics to be considered by a CKMS designer when developing a CKMS design specification. Topics include security policies, cryptographic keys and metadata, interoperability and transitioning, security controls, testing and system assurances, disaster recovery, and security assessments.
SP 800-131A	Special Publication 800-131A Revision 1, *Transitions: Recommendation for Transitioning the Use of Cryptographic Algorithms and Key Lengths*, November 2015. http://dx.doi.org/10.6028/NIST.SP.800-131Ar1 Section 5.6.4 of SP 800-57, Part 1 provides recommendations for transitioning to new cryptographic algorithms and key lengths because of algorithm breaks or the availability of more powerful computers that could be used to efficiently search for cryptographic keys. SP 800-131A offers more specific guidance for such transitions. Each algorithm and service is addressed in SP 800-131A, indicating whether its use is acceptable, deprecated, restricted, allowed only for legacy applications[77], or disallowed.
SP 800-132	Special Publication 800-132, *Recommendation for Password-Based Key Derivation, Part 1: Storage Applications*, December 2010. http://dx.doi.org/10.6028/NIST.SP.800-132 SP 800-132 specifies techniques for the derivation of master keys from passwords or passphrases to protect stored electronic data or data protection keys.
SP 800-133	Special Publication 800-133, *Recommendation for Cryptographic Key Generation*, December 2012. http://dx.doi.org/10.6028/NIST.SP.800-133 SP 800-133 discusses the generation of the keys to be managed and used by the **approved** cryptographic algorithms.

---

[77] The algorithm and key length may be used to process already-protected information, but there may be a risk in doing so.

SP 800-135	Special Publication 800-135 Revision 1, *Recommendation for Existing Application-Specific Key Derivation Functions*, December 2011. http://dx.doi.org/10.6028/NIST.SP.800-135r1 Many widely-used internet security protocols have their own application-specific Key Derivation Functions (KDFs) that are used to generate the cryptographic keys required for their cryptographic functions. SP 800-135 provides security requirements for those KDFs.
SP 800-152	Special Publication 800-152, *A Profile for U. S. Federal Cryptographic Key Management Systems (CKMS)*, October 2015. http://dx.doi.org/10.6028/NIST.SP.800-152 SP 800-152 contains requirements for the design, implementation, procurement, installation, configuration, management, operation and use of a CKMS by and for U.S. federal organizations and their contractors. The Profile is based on NIST Special Publication SP 800-130.
SP 800-175A	Special Publication 800-175A, *Guideline for Using Cryptographic Standards in the Federal Government: Directives, Mandates and Policies*, August 2016. http://dx.doi.org/10.6028/NIST.SP.800-175A SP 800-175A provides guidance on the determination of requirements for using cryptography. It includes a summary of laws and regulations concerning the protection of the Federal Government's sensitive information, guidance regarding the conduct of risk assessments to determine what needs to be protected and how best to protect that information, and a discussion of the relevant security-related documents (e.g., various policy and practice documents).
NISTIR 7924	NIST Internal Report 7924 (Second Draft), *Reference Security Policy*, May 2014. http://csrc.nist.gov/publications/PubsDrafts.html#NIST-IR-7924 [accessed 8/18/16]. NIST 7924 is intended to identify a set of security controls and practices to support the secure issuance of certificates. It was written in the form of a Certificate Policy (CP), a standard format for defining the expectations and requirements of the relying party community that will trust the certificates issued by its Certificate Authorities (CAs).

Non-NIST Publications:

IEEE 802.11	*Wireless Local Area Networks* [web page]. http://standards.ieee.org/about/get/802/802.11.html
IEEE P1363	IEEE P1363: *Standard Specifications for Public-Key Cryptography* [web page]. http://grouper.ieee.org/groups/1363/
IEEE P1363a	IEEE P1363a: *Standard Specifications For Public Key Cryptography-Amendment 1: Additional Techniques*, 2004.
IEEE P1363.1	*Public-Key Cryptographic Techniques Based on Hard Problems over Lattices*, October 2008.
IEEE P1363.2	*Password-Based Public-Key Cryptography*, 2008.
IEEE P1619	*Standard for Cryptographic Protection of Data on Block-Oriented Storage Devices*, 2008.
ISO/IEC 9594-8	ITU-T Recommendation X.509 (2012) | ISO/IEC 9594-8:2014, *Information technology - Open Systems Interconnection - The Directory: Public-key and attribute certificate frameworks*.
ISO/IEC 9797-1	ISO/IEC 9797-1:2011, *Information technology − Security techniques − Message Authentication Codes (MACs) − Part 1: Mechanisms using a block cipher*, March 2011. This standard includes CMAC, as specified in SP 800-38B.
ISO/IEC 9797-2	ISO/IEC 9797-2:2011, *Information technology − Security techniques − Message Authentication Codes (MACs) − Part 2: Mechanisms using a dedicated hash-function*, May 2011. This standard includes HMAC, as specified in FIPS 198.
ISO/IEC 10116	ISO/IEC 10116:2006, *Information technology − Security techniques − Modes of operation for an n-bit block cipher*, February 2006. This standard includes all the modes specified in SP 800-38A.
ISO/IEC 10118-3	ISO/IEC 10118-3:2004, *Information technology − Security techniques − Hash-functions − Part 3: Dedicated hash-functions*, March 2004. This standard includes SHA-1 and the SHA-2 family of hash functions specified in FIPS 180. A revision of ISO/IEC 10118-3 will

	include the SHA-3 functions specified in FIPS 202.
ISO/IEC 11770-3	ISO/IEC 11770-3: 2015, *Information technology − Security techniques − Key management -- Part 3: Mechanisms using asymmetric techniques*, August 2015. This standard specifies key establishment mechanisms, some of which can be instantiated with key-establishment schemes specified in SP 800-56A and SP 800-56B.
ISO/IEC FDIS 11770-6	ISO/IEC FDIS 11770-6, *Information technology − Security techniques − Key management − Part 6: Key derivation*, 2015. This draft standard will include all key derivation functions specified in SP 800-108, as well as the two-step key derivation methods specified in SP 800-56C.
ISO/IEC 11889	ISO/IEC 11889-1:2015, *Information technology − Trusted Platform Module Library − Part 1: Architecture*, August 2015. ISO/IEC 11889-2:2015, *Information technology − Trusted Platform Module − Part 2: Structures*, August 2015. ISO/IEC 11889-3:2015, *Information technology − Trusted Platform Module − Part 3: Commands*, August 2015. ISO/IEC 11889-4:2015, *Information technology − Trusted Platform Module Library − Part 4: Supporting Routines*, August 2015.
ISO/IEC 14888-2	ISO/IEC 14888-2:2008, *Information technology − Security techniques − Digital signatures with appendix − Part 2: Integer factorization based mechanisms*, April 2008. This standard includes RSA signatures, as specified in FIPS 186.
ISO/IEC 14888-3	ISO/IEC 14888-3:2016, *Information technology − Security techniques − Digital signatures with appendix − Part 3: Discrete logarithm based mechanisms*, March 2016. This standard includes DSA, as specified for finite fields and elliptic curves in FIPS 186.
ISO/IEC 18033-3	ISO/IEC 18033-3:2010, *Information technology − Security techniques − Encryption algorithms − Part 3: Block ciphers*, December 2010. This standard includes 64-bit block ciphers: TDEA, MISTY1, CAST-128, HIGHT and 128-bit block ciphers: AES, Camellia, and SEED. Note that TDEA is specified in SP 800-67 and AES is specified in FIPS 197.

ISO/IEC 19772	ISO/IEC 19772:2009, *Information technology – Security techniques – Authenticated encryption*, February 2009.
	This standard includes CCM (as specified in SP 800-38C), GCM (as specified in SP 800-38D), and Key wrapping (as specified in SP 800-38E).
PKCS 1	Public Key Cryptography System #1, version 2.2, *RSA Cryptography Standard*, October 27, 2012.
	http://www.emc.com/emc-plus/rsa-labs/pkcs/files/h11300-wp-pkcs-1v2-2-rsa-cryptography-standard.pdf [accessed 8/18/16].
	PKCS 1 provides recommendations for the implementation of public-key cryptography based on the RSA algorithm, covering cryptographic primitives, encryption schemes, signature schemes with appendix and the ASN.1 syntax for representing keys and for identifying the schemes.
X9.31	American National Standard for Financial Services X9.31-1998, *Digital Signatures Using Reversible Public Key Cryptography for the Financial Services Industry (rDSA)*, 1998 [withdrawn].
	ANS X9.31 defined a method for digital signature (signature) generation and verification for the protection of financial messages and data using reversible public key cryptography systems without message recovery. In addition, criteria for the generation of public and private keys required by the algorithm and the procedural controls required for the secure use of the algorithm were provided.
X9.42	American National Standard for Financial Services X9.42-2001, *Public Key Cryptography for the Financial Services Industry: Agreement of Symmetric Keys Using Discrete Logarithm Cryptography*, 2001 [withdrawn].
	ANS X9.42, partially adapted from ISO 11770-3, specifies schemes for the agreement of symmetric keys using the Diffie-Hellman and MQV algorithms. It covers methods for domain-parameter generation, domain-parameter validation, key-pair generation, public-key validation, shared secret value calculation, key derivation, and test message authentication code computation for discrete-logarithm problem-based key-agreement schemes.

X9.44	American National Standard for Financial Services X9.44-2007, *Key Establishment Using Integer Factorization Cryptography*, 2007. ANS X9.44 specifies key-establishment schemes using public-key cryptography, based on the integer factorization problem. Two types of key-establishment schemes are specified: key transport and key agreement.
X9.62	American National Standard X9.62-2005, *Public Key Cryptography for the Financial Services Industry: the Elliptic Curve Digital Signature Algorithm (ECDSA)*, 2005. ANS X9.62 defines methods for digital signature (signature) generation and verification for the protection of messages and data using the Elliptic Curve Digital Signature Algorithm (ECDSA). This Standard provides methods and criteria for the generation of public and private keys that are required by ECDSA and the procedural controls required for the secure use of the algorithm with these keys. This ECDSA Standard also provides methods and criteria for the generation of elliptic-curve domain parameters that are required by ECDSA and the procedural controls required for the secure use of the algorithm with these domain parameters.
X9.63	American National Standard X9.63-2011, *Public Key Cryptography for the Financial Services Industry: Key Agreement and Key Transport Using Elliptic Curve Cryptography*, 2011. ANS X9.63 defines key-establishment schemes that employ asymmetric cryptographic techniques. The arithmetic operations involved in the operation of the schemes take place in the algebraic structure of an elliptic curve over a finite field. Both key-agreement and key-transport schemes are specified.

www.ingramcontent.com/pod-product-compliance
Lightning Source LLC
Chambersburg PA
CBHW082122070326
40690CB00049B/4114